Hitler's Gauls

The History of the 33rd Waffen-Grenadier Division der SS (französische Nr 1) Charlemagne

Book 1 in the Hitler's Legions series

HITLER'S GAULS

THE HISTORY OF THE 33RD WAFFEN-GRENADIER DIVISION

DER SS (FRANZÖSISCHE NR 1) CHARLEMAGNE

Book 1 in the *Hitler's Legions* series

by

Jonathan Trigg

SPELLMOUNT

First published in 2006
This edition published in 2009

By Spellmount, an imprint of
The History Press
The Mill, Brimscombe Port
Stroud, Gloucestershire, GL5 2QG
www.thehistorypress.co.uk

British Library Cataloguing in Publication Data.
A catalogue record for this book is available from the British Library.

ISBN 978 0 7524 5476 4

Typesetting and origination by The History Press
Printed in Great Britain

Contents

List of Maps

Acknowledgements

The author would like to express his thanks to a number of people, without whose help and support this book would never have been written. First to the Charlemagne veterans, André Bayle and Gilbert Gilles, who took the time to humour an obsessive Englishman, and to Anthony 'Gurkha' Corbett and Katie Monach who spent many hours translating all the author's correspondence to and from the said veterans to make up for his truly appalling French. To Frau Notzke at the Bundesarchiv who patiently helped find material when I wasn't being very specific, to my editor, David, and Kim at Spellmount who put up with endless stupid questions, and to my publisher, Jamie, a straight batter if ever there was one, thank you. To Tim Shaw, a reproduction wizard and a true friend, again thank you. Lastly to my wife, as beautiful as she is patient, she has managed to feign interest in this project for almost two years, and for that I thank her.

Acknowledgements

Introduction

The nightmare was finally at an end. The evil of Adolf Hitler and Nazism was burning in the vast funeral pyre that was the capital of the much-vaunted 'Thousand Year Reich'. Smiling and joyful Red Army soldiers watched as Sergeants M A Yegorov and M V Kantaria from the Soviet 150th Rifle Division triumphantly hoisted the hammer and sickle Red Banner No.5 on the rear parapet of the ruined Reichstag on the afternoon of 2 May 1945. That image of victory was caught on camera for publication all over the world. This symbolic act established beyond doubt the total victory of Soviet Russia over Nazi Germany. Although as was so often the case in Stalin's Machiavellian world, the truth was not as represented to the world; it later transpired that the first soldier to raise a Soviet flag over the Reichstag building was in fact an artillery captain more than twelve hours earlier than officially recognised. It was decided at the time however that the photo taken of that event lacked the proper background to establish the site in the audience's mind, so the official Soviet war photographer selected the rear parapet as the site and Sergeants Yegorov and Kantaria as suitably 'proletarian Soviet' heroes for the now-famous picture.

For Soviet Russia the fact that the Reichstag itself had been closed since the infamous fire of 1933 was irrelevant. Final German armed resistance might well have been concentrated around the Chancellery building and the Führer Bunker in its garden, but for the Soviet people at home waiting desperately for news of final victory, the Reichstag was the ultimate symbol of Nazi Germany, and to see it humbled was to finally know the war in Europe was over.

Below the antics of staged propaganda cinematography there were long, though as a vivid reflection of the bitterness of the fighting, not over-long columns of defeated German soldiers, sailors and airmen winding their way slowly and dejectedly through the rubble-strewn streets and into the uncertain tender mercies of Soviet captivity. Many of the faces of those defeated soldiers were of old men, the last remnants of Germany's citizen home guard, the Volkssturm, thrown into battle by the crumbling

Nazi Party hierarchy in a last desperate attempt to stave off final defeat. Most heartbreaking of all though, particularly for the surviving civilians of Berlin watching the pathetic end of the drama, were the columns of boys from the Hitler Youth being marched away to the horrors of the gulags. These boys, some as young as 12 or 13, dressed in scraps of ill-fitting and oversized uniforms, had been called to action alongside their grandfathers in the Volkssturm and were now paying the price of their futile resistance. For so many the rubble of Berlin would be their last sight of Germany. Few would ever return to their homeland alive.

But not all in the defeated Nazi ranks were grey-haired grandfathers or beardless boys. Some were hard-faced young men with the still proud bearing of Germany's feared and respected *'Frontschwein'*, combat veterans, and it was one of these that a drunken Red Army soldier singled out from his comrades and pulled out of line. The Soviet soldier screamed accusingly at his defeated enemy the same phrase that Russian soldiers, and indeed civilians, had come to fear and loathe since the invasion of the Soviet Union in 1941, 'SS, SS'. But before the Russian could do anything about his accusation the singled out soldier was pulled away from his grasp and hustled back into line by yet another Russian guard. The relieved POW turned to his fellow captives and said with a sigh of relief, 'That was a narrow escape!', only for the drunken Russian to grab him again, pull him to one side away from his comrades, shove a pistol against his forehead and pull the trigger. He was dead before he hit the ground. In the orgy of conquest common to most victorious armies in history, this incident was sadly commonplace and, unfortunately in respect of human life, hardly worthy of historical note, except for certain facts.

The first was that the Russian soldier singled out that captive deliberately; this was no random act of savagery. The murdered man was not executed for *who* he was but rather for *what* he was, a member of an organisation that had carved its name in blood across the Russian steppes, the SS. In this regard the Russian was correct in his identification at least; the murdered soldier was indeed SS, in fact a Waffen-SS Unterscharführer, a full corporal. Secondly, and of critical interest, is the fact that the Unterscharführer didn't speak to his comrades moments before his death in German, but in French. In fact the murdered man wasn't German at all, but a Frenchman; his name was Roger Albert-Brunet, a native of Dauphine and a winner of the Iron Cross 1st Class, and he wasn't the only Frenchman there from the Waffen-SS in the burning ruins of Berlin.

With the European phase of World War II finally over, Berlin had become a battlefield in common with dozens of cities across Western and Eastern Europe and the Soviet Union. And like Leningrad, Minsk, Warsaw and Rotterdam, it too had paid the price in fire and ruin. Like so many urban landscapes of the previous six years, the German capital was dotted with the debris of modern warfare. Around the shattered buildings and scattered throughout the wrecked city lay the burning hulks of Russian tanks and self-propelled guns, destroyed mainly by small bands of tank busters operating on foot and armed with nothing more sophisticated than handheld anti-tank weapons, the ubiquitous Panzerfäusts, a simple metal tube with a hollow charge attached and a range of less than 100 metres. Heaps of dead Soviet infantrymen lay thickly strewn up and down the once beautiful Berlin streets, testament that though the battle was short it was also savage and cost the Red Army dear. Indeed Soviet casualties in the taking of Berlin totalled 78,291 men killed and 274,184 wounded, and this against an enemy in its death throes.

So was this desperate defence the last throw of the much-vaunted German Aryan superman? The racial German *Herrenvolk*? Actually no, many of these diehard defenders fighting on to the bitter end were non-Germans: Balts, Norwegians, Danes, Swedes and Frenchmen. These latter were the remnants of the 33rd Waffen-Grenadier-Division der SS (französische Nr.1) Charlemagne. French Waffen-SS men?

In a century dominated by strident nationalism how and why were soldiers of half-a-dozen different nationalities fighting to the last man for a regime that had invaded most of their homelands and was undoubtedly one of the most bloodstained and horrific in history? For the French grenadiers in particular, how could countrymen of the victims of atrocities such as Tulle and Oradour-sur-Glane wear the hated lightning flashes, the pagan *sig* runes of the Waffen-SS, until the very end? From where did they come? Why did they do what they did? What is their story?

CHAPTER I

France: The Rise of the Extreme Right

The road to a murdered French Waffen-SS volunteer in a burning Berlin began decades earlier in the mud and slaughter of the Western Front in World War I. The years of carnage in the trenches dominated post-World War I France, and led to twenty-one years of political and social turmoil that created the breeding ground from which Charlemagne, and the men who served in it, would spring.

The end of the war to end all wars saw France emerge victorious, but exhausted. With her Allies she had defeated Prussian militarism, and regained the provinces of Alsace-Lorraine lost after her defeat in the Franco-Prussian War forty-seven years earlier. However, the price had been extraordinarily high. France had lost over one-and-a-half million men killed and more than four million wounded; the war had mainly been fought on her soil and much of northern France was laid waste. In human terms France's national consciousness was to be forever haunted by the multitude of monuments to her fallen that sprang up in every city, town and village in the land.

Post-war chaos

The post-war political chaos that infested so many nations, Germany and the new Communist Russia being prominent among them, also resonated in France. Between 1918 and 1940 France had forty-two separate governments, lasting on average just six months. In the three years from 1932 to 1935 alone, there were eleven different administrations presiding over fourteen 'national economic recovery plans'. Chronic political insecurity and instability led many in France, just as in neighbouring Germany, to look to the political extremes of the far Left and Right for the answers. In France communism found a ready home in a nation with a long tradition of working-class radicalism and revolution. After all France was the setting for the storming of the Bastille and the Paris Commune. Balancing the growth of the far Left was the explosion of support for the splintered politics of the far Right. Here aristocratic monarchists rubbed shoulders with working-class nationalists, representatives of big business and a bourgeoisie desperate for stability and order. This conglomeration of the unlikely found particular expression in the founding of mass membership political organisations, often with paramilitary overtones.

The largest and most influential organisation was L'Action Française, an umbrella grouping for right-wingers of all shades and hues, with a strong pro-monarchist streak. This organisation was founded by the leading French thinker, Charles Maurras, but it was by no means the only group on the far Right. There was a proliferation of rightist organisations, such as the ex-French Army Colonel de la Roque's Croix de Feu, mainly made up Great War veterans, or for those more dedicated to the extremes of armed action there were the shadowy paramilitaries of Eugène Deloncle's Comité Secret d'Action Révolutionnaire, better known as Les Cagoulards, the Hooded Ones. Young people were accommodated in the champagne magnate Pierre Taittinger's Jeunesses Patriotes founded in 1924, a movement with echoes of the yet-to-be-born Hitler Youth, and while there is no doubt that there was a great deal of overlap in membership, it is also clear that the far Right in France at the time was a mass movement with genuine popular support.

Though nowhere near as violent as the corresponding situation in Germany, where right-wing veterans of the Great War joined the freebooting Freikorps bands and fought a virtual civil war with their enemies of the Left, street violence became commonplace in France's cities and added to the general feeling of chaos and dissatisfaction that successive governments were unable to deal with. Confidence in the Republic's establishment and the body politic was low and nothing seemed to be able to reverse the decline. When large numbers of mainstream politicians were implicated in the infamous Stavisky Affair in February 1934, so-named for the Ukrainian Jewish fraudster at the centre of the financial scandal, L'Action Française incited street riots and its supporters invaded the National Assembly building in Paris. The bloody street fighting between the police and right-wingers on the night of 6 February 1934 left six people dead and over 655 others in hospital. The reverberations of the violence were felt all over France, and in the shocked aftermath the Republic acted to protect itself by banning a host of politically motivated organisations that were not officially designated as political parties. This heavy handed approach was a conspicuous failure. The Croix de Feu for instance was banned only to resurface as the official Parti Social Français (PSF) with an official membership of 800,000 by 1936. The formation of the leftist Popular Front Government in 1936 under the Prime Minister, Léon Blum, only served to inflame the bigotries of the extreme Right and unite its disparate factions in opposition, particularly as Blum was Jewish. He himself was to remain a focus for right-wing hatred until the outbreak of World War II and the extreme Right could exact its revenge.

Extremist ideology and politics

The growth of the far Right in France was not purely in the arena of popular political activism. It was also given succour by certain strands of French intellectualism. France has a long tradition, unlike Great Britain for instance, of attaching huge importance to the thinking of its own home-grown intellectuals, and of that same thinking having a far-reaching influence on the mainstream population. Several of the French intellectual elite of the day were at the forefront of the Europe-wide *fin de siècle* intellectual movement whose ideas of a unique European cultural heritage and the growing threat from the East found a ready home on the political extreme Right in France. Recurrent themes written and debated about were the supposed weaknesses and decadence of the European liberal democratic model of government, and the twin perceived threats of international communism and Jewish-controlled capitalism. The intellectuals' solution was a pan-European alliance that would combat the alleged tide of barbarism from the East that threatened to engulf Europe's unique cultural inheritance. These same thinkers believed that Europe needed a revival, a rebirth, and, crucially, that this was not going to be a French-centred act but rather a 'European' one. When World War II came it was seen by them and their supporters as a fight to preserve European culture, values and heritage, as well as European hegemony. One French writer who later became an active collaborator, Pierre Drieu la Rochelle, wrote as early as 1922 in his *Mesure de la France*:

> ...we must create a United States of Europe, because it is the only way of defending Europe against itself and against other human groups.

Such writings gave extreme Right political parties an intellectual legitimacy they had previously been lacking and helped them to flourish. While the banning of organisations such as the Croix de Feu only served to channel their members into active participation in legitimate political parties.

Jacques Doriot

The Parti Social Français might have had a membership of close to a million, but it was not the largest or most influential pre-war party of the extreme Right in France. That position went to the Parti Populaire Français (the PPF), led by the well-known and charismatic politician, Jacques Doriot. Doriot was a typical far Right leader of his day with a political pedigree that began in the theatre of working-class struggle on the Left before moving inexorably to the Right. In this he unthinkingly aped the far better known Italian dictator, Benito Mussolini, himself a figure who began on the Italian extreme political Left to finally end up as Italy's fascist supremo. Doriot was born on 26 September 1898 at Bresles, in the department of Oise. He moved to Paris in 1915 and became a labourer in the industrial Parisian suburb of Saint-Denis. He joined the Jeunesses Socialistes de France (the Socialist Youth of France) in 1916 aged 17, and was then mobilised the following year to serve in the trenches where he won the Croix de Guerre in combat. He was subsequently captured by the Germans and held prisoner until the armistice.

On his repatriation to France, Doriot joined the newly-formed French Communist Party in 1920 and thereafter rose rapidly through its ranks, becoming a member of the presidium of the executive committee of the Communist Internationale in 1922, Secretary of the French Federation of Young Communists in 1923, then serving a short sentence in La Santé prison in Paris for opposition to Poincaré's occupation of the Ruhr, before being elected to the Chamber of Deputies to represent the Seine region in 1924. After a period in the Chamber he confirmed his ascendancy by being elected to the politically powerful position of Mayor of Saint-Denis in 1931. In French political life a mayoralty is highly sought after (the current French President Jacques Chirac based his drive for presidential power on his mayoralty of Paris), and this post enabled Doriot to establish a political power base independent of the Communist Party, giving him control over his own private fiefdom in the heart of the French capital.

Prior to his election Doriot had withdrawn from the leadership of the French Communist Party over his doubts as to the rigidly held dogma of a Communist Party-only ticket to achieve political power. But it was while Mayor of Saint-Denis that he began to openly discuss the possibility of alliances with other leftist parties as part of a coalition for power. This was heresy to the Communist Party apparatchiks, and he was expelled from the Party in June 1934. Their reasoning was clear: Doriot's pragmatic approach clashed with the Party line that decreed that the Communists were the only standard bearers of the workers and all other parties were actually pseudo-bourgeois. The expulsion was a bitter blow for Doriot personally. He saw it as a rejection by the Party he had served all his political life, but he refused to leave politics and decided instead to remain in the Chamber of Deputies and form his own party which would be based on his ideas and political leadership.

Thus was born the PPF on 22 June 1936. Expansion was rapid and PPF membership soon topped 250,000. As the party grew Doriot increasingly shifted ideologically to the Right and unsurprisingly became a virulent anti-Communist; in this it is hard not to see a great deal of personal bitterness against his former comrades. Doriot began espousing fascism, expressing admiration for Mussolini in particular, and he also used the Party paper, *Le Cri du Peuple (The Cry of the People)*, to advocate collaboration with Europe's other rising political and economic star, Nazi Germany, whose seeming resurgence under Hitler greatly impressed him. In the apparent rebirth of Italy and Germany Doriot saw France's future; a future where she would reaffirm her place as one of the pre-eminent nations in the world in her new form as a fascist state.

The PSF and the PPF were the largest of the pre-war French political parties of the far Right but they were far from alone. Indeed the far Right of the political spectrum in France was remarkably crowded with a host of minor parties that came and went, but not until the former cabinet minister Marcel Déat's Rassemblement National Populaire (RNP) was established on 1 February 1941, was there anything of the same magnitude as the PSF or the PPF. While often bitterly bickering amongst themselves, what these parties actually did was establish a popular acceptance and legitimacy in France of the far Right and its thinking. For many party members, particularly the youngest, often the most idealistic and committed, this meant a glamorisation of Hitler's Germany in particular, and the ideal of a pan-European future as opposed to a purely French one. These seeds were sown on fertile ground in France and such supra-national thinking was to lead directly to the creation of Charlemagne.

Joseph Darnard

Doriot was the leading party political figure who impacted greatly on French opinion, and who helped sow the seeds that would later lead to Frenchmen fighting it out with the Red Army in Berlin's burning ruins. But outside this purely political influence, the best known, and now most infamous figure, was undoubtedly Joseph Darnard.

Born on 19 March 1897 in Coligny of humble stock, his father was a railway worker, the patriotic young Joseph joined the 35e régiment d'infanterie of the French Army on the outbreak of World War I and went on to serve with distinction, winning no fewer than seven separate citations for bravery and specialising in leading daring groups of raiders into German-held territory. After the War he applied for a regular commission to continue his move up the ladder of military promotion; however he was refused, and somewhat disillusioned at what he saw as a snub, decided to leave the Army altogether and pursue an alternative career. He became a cabinet maker initially and then set up his own highly successful transport company operating out of Nice. Whilst building his business Darnard became active in politics, supporting the royalist L'Action Française like many of his fellow Great War veterans.

During his time as a supporter of L'Action Française Darnard began to associate with the more extreme fringes of the organisation and eventually he graduated into hard core militant activity, particularly with the secretive Cagoulards. In support of this shadowy paramilitary group Darnard used his business activities as a cover to smuggle weapons into the country from abroad and eventually became their chief in Nice. The smuggled arms were stockpiled in a series of secret locations to be used by Les Cagoulards against what they perceived to be any threats to the nation, the greatest of which was their fear of an internal communist-led insurgency and an ensuing civil war. Given his escalating involvement with the militants it was only a matter of time before Darnard's activities came to the attention of the police and security services. That moment finally came when he was implicated in the murder of a low-level criminal, Maurice Juif, who was said to have double-crossed Les Cagoulards. Darnard was arrested, questioned and detained for six months by the police, but subsequently released with an off-the-record warning to halt further activity unless he wanted to end up in prison again. In the aftermath of this lucky escape Darnard wound down his involvement with Les Cagoulards and bided his time.

CHAPTER II

Germany: The Birth of the Waffen-SS

In Germany the political earthquake had already happened, and now standing guard at the Chancellery were black-clad giants of the Waffen-SS, staring impassively forward. The Waffen-SS? Who were they? Where did they come from? What was the tradition from which they sprang? The key to understanding this hitherto unknown organisation and its subsequent growth lay in Germany's past.

Germany is born

Prussia's Iron Chancellor, Otto von Bismarck, created Imperial Germany from a multiplicity of Germanic mini-states, and that nationhood was made possible by war with the key battles being fought in the Austro-Prussian and Franco-Prussian Wars at the end of the 19th century.

This Germany, a country born in the unification wars and possessing huge economic and military muscle, had challenged the established imperial countries of France, Great Britain and Russia in a bid to join their ranks as a Great Power in the world. This challenge led to World War I, the mud and death of the Marne, Tannenberg, Verdun, the Somme and Ypres, and finally to Germany's capitulation and the ignominy of the Versailles Treaty. Germany's humiliation was felt most keenly on the issue of land. Denmark and Belgium benefited from their annexation of Schleswig-Holstein and the Eupen-Malmédy regions respectively, and the resurrected state of Poland was given access to the Baltic Sea via a land corridor through Germany with the Free City of Danzig at its head. For France the disputed provinces of Alsace-Lorraine (annexed by a victorious Prussia at the end of the Franco-Prussian War in 1871) were returned. To add to this burden Germany was humbled economically with the imposition of huge sums to be paid in war reparations. The Spanish flu pandemic then ravaged a war-weary German population weakened physically by years of food shortages brought on by the successful British naval blockade. This was followed by the global

21

Great Depression with hyperinflation and the near collapse of the entire financial system in Germany. The result was a German state in near total meltdown. In less than twenty years Germany had lost the largest war ever fought in world history, several millions of its people through war, hunger and disease, and been brought to the verge of complete economic collapse. Politically these conditions were the basis for Hitler's rise.

On the military front the once-proud Imperial German Army and military machine was emasculated by the terms of the Versailles Treaty. The newly-established German Army, the Reichswehr, was capped at no more than 100,000 men, a number considered adequate for defence. The Reichswehr was also denied emergent military technologies with a ban on possession of any armoured vehicles including tanks. Germany was prohibited from having an air force for the Reichswehr to operate with, and her navy, the Kriegsmarine, was limited to having ships of less than 10,000 tonnes displacement. However from the date of the Treaty's signing the German High Command had seen its mission to be finding ways around the restrictions. Results included a strategy for the Kriegsmarine based on U-boats and 'pocket battleships', a new Luftwaffe secretly trained in Soviet Russia and an Army structured as a basis for rapid expansion. Hitler's reassurances to the generals that the restrictions imposed by Versailles would be progressively dismantled ensured their support in his bid for power, and indeed on Hitler's election to the Chancellorship on 30 January 1933 he immediately began a process of rapid rearmament that flouted Versailles to the benefit of the armed forces. This policy though did not solve all the issues between the Army and the Nazis. Indeed this relationship between the two dominant institutions in German life would remain a source of huge tension until after the 20 July 1944 bomb plot against Hitler. The aftermath of that unsuccessful assassination attempt would finally see the last vestiges of army independence broken in the show trials of high ranking officers conducted by the Nazi state prosecutor, Roland Freisler.

The coming of the Nazis and the Brown Shirts

In the chaos of the Weimar Republic years the politics of the day became heavily radicalised. There was no centrist consensus and the parties of the extreme Right and Left flourished. Political violence was commonplace and widespread. Communist Party supporters regularly fought it out in the streets with supporters of the biggest extreme right-wing party, Adolf Hitler's National Sozialistische Deutsche Arbeiter Partei (NSDAP), the Nazis. At the time politics revolved around the hustings, with politicians touring the country drumming up support at rallies both big and small. Supporters of rival parties often attended to disrupt the speeches and physically attack the speakers. Informally at first groups of men were formed to protect speakers. For the Nazis this saw the foundation of the ubiquitous Brown Shirts of the SA, the Sturmabteilung, storm troopers.

The SA was led by one of Hitler's oldest and closest friends and political allies, Ernst Röhm. This burly ex-soldier saw the Nazi mission as one of creating a new social order in Germany, one where the power of the army and the industrialists was replaced by a true mass social revolution that would be led by the Nazi Party with his brown-shirted storm troopers in the vanguard. From humble beginnings the SA grew from a handful of men to almost three million members by the end of 1933. Invaluable when the Party was vying for power, on his accession to the Chancellorship the SA became an embarrassment to Hitler and a bone of contention in his relationship with the generals. In 1933 the army was still the one institution capable of standing up to the Nazis and so needed to be placated. This was becoming increasingly difficult due to Röhm's loud and public advocacy of the eventual replacement of the army by the SA, and his growing impatience to begin his promised 'revolution'.

Men in black: the SS
In order to remove the problem once and for all Hitler turned to the Nazis' other private army, the SS. Established originally as the Stabswache, or Staff Guard, to protect Hitler personally, the unit initially consisted of just two men, Josef Berchtold and Julius Schreck. It evolved into the Stosstrupp Adolf Hitler, and then finally the Protection Squad, in German the Shützstaffel, or SS. During its various transitions it came under the leadership of a man who seemingly excelled only in his ordinariness. Bespectacled, of medium height and physically unprepossessing, with a reputation as a competent Nazi Party administrator in his native Bavaria, Heinrich Himmler was in reality anything but ordinary. Much has been written about Himmler and why such a seemingly inconsequential man could become the monster he undoubtedly was. A particularly good description of the enigma that was Himmler was written by the sometime diplomat and journalist Edward Crankshaw:

He was not distinguished by cruelty, by lust, by excessive vanity, by overweening ambition, by systematic deceitfulness. His qualities were unremarkable, vices and virtues alike. But there was no centre: the qualities simply did not cohere.

There are men like Himmler in the prisons and criminal lunatic asylums all over the world – and, more unfortunately placed by virtue of the possession of private incomes, leading retired and slightly dotty lives in seaside bungalows along our coasts. They are the sort of men, good husbands and fathers, kind to animals, gentle, hesitant, soft-spoken, absorbed in some mild hobby and probably very good at it, who murder their wives because they wish to marry another girl and flinch from the scandal of a divorce.[1]

Himmler epitomised the unremarkable face of evil, but Hitler saw in him the one quality he prized above all others, loyalty, and in time Himmler was to become referred to by Hitler as '*der treue Heinrich*'. He would keep this soubriquet until the last month of the war when his master found out about his futile peace feelers through the Red Cross's Swedish envoy, Count Folke Bernadotte.

Himmler was fascinated by the occult, herbalism, Germanic paganism and genetic racial theory and he would prove to have an exceptional talent for both organisation and conspiracy. In the SS Himmler saw the means of his own rise to power. Eventually the organisation he created and controlled would become, in effect, a state within a state in Germany, and the key to that was the formation of armed units.

The creation of such an armed force, independent of the army, was not uncommon in continental Europe, where many countries were long used to armed police forces and even paramilitary units designed to combat civil unrest. In this context the formation by the German government, as the Nazi Party had become, of a small paramilitary formation did not seem out of place. The fact that this formation was entirely at the personal disposal of the Führer and utterly obedient to him, and not the institutions of the state, was nothing more than an administrative issue as far as most Germans were concerned.

This idea of a 'political army', however, has always been difficult to understand in countries where the army is the only legitimate institution of the state allowed to bear arms, and is strictly separate from politics. In the UK for instance witness even now the discomfort and alarm felt by most of the population at the prospect of selectively arming police officers on a regular basis. The notion of a party political leader, such as Churchill or Attlee, forming armed groups would have been total anathema and utterly incomprehensible.

Night of the Long Knives
It was precisely these 'administrative circumstances' though that allowed Hitler to lance the boil of Röhm and the SA. On 30 June 1934 SS formations left their barracks to break the power of the SA once and for all in the 'Night of the Long Knives'. The premier SS formation, the Leibstandarte Adolf Hitler under its commander Josep 'Sepp' Dietrich, left its barracks in Berlin Lichterfelde and headed for the Bavarian spa resort town of Bad Wiessee where Röhm had gathered many of his SA leaders for a

relaxing conference. Their orders were clear. Round up the SA leaders and then shoot them immediately. Röhm himself was arrested and offered the opportunity to commit suicide; in total disbelief at the situation he refused and was shot dead by his erstwhile comrade Theodor Eicke (later commander of the 3rd SS Panzer Division Totenkopf). Most of the senior SA leadership nationwide was murdered, many of them shouting 'Heil Hitler' as they faced the firing squads, believing they were victims of an SS plot to overthrow the Führer – misplaced loyalty indeed. Following this act of Nazi fratricide the SS was allowed to expand by a grateful Hitler.

The organisation became an independent arm of the Nazi Party, no longer subject to the control of the SA as it had been up until then. In a decree of September 1934, Hitler outlined the main task of the new force. Trained on military lines, it was to be ready for a fanatical war of ideology that would break out within Germany should the regime's opponents rebel. Only in the event of general war would it be employed for military purposes, in which case only Hitler could decide how and when it would be used. The Reichswehr was not entirely comfortable with the arrangement but Field Marshal Blomberg, the Defence Minister, was reassured by Hitler that the intention was to create an armed police force and not another army. This reassurance, like so many of Hitler's, proved entirely false.

Himmler's fantasy: the new Teutonic knights

Himmler, now officially entitled Reichsführer-SS, patiently went about fulfilling the fantasy he had constructed in his own mind for the future of the Waffen-SS. Himmler's fervent imaginings foresaw a German Empire dominant in Europe with huge colonies in the Lebensraum, living space, of the East. These colonies would be manned by a new breed of 'warrior-farmers', tall, robust, blond haired and blue-eyed Aryans, dedicated to the establishment of the Nazi ideal and the destruction of Bolshevism and Jewry. This new order of Teutonic centurions would have the Waffen-SS as its vanguard. Sired by 'pure' Aryan bloodlines and forged in the cauldron of battle the Waffen-SS would symbolise the zenith of Nazism and be a potent display of its victory over the so-called inferior races. Incredible as it seems now, it would be this lurid vision that would see non-Aryan Frenchmen fighting in Berlin under the banner of the Waffen-SS a scant decade later.

The Waffen-SS began to emerge rapidly as an organisation following the purge of the SA, and was formed at its core around three distinct units. First was Hitler's personal bodyguard unit, the elite Leibstandarte. An independent force even within the SS, the Leibstandarte was known firstly for its incredibly strict entrance criteria; Himmler's boast was that a single filled tooth disqualified a candidate, and secondly its ill-deserved reputation as 'asphalt soldiers' due to its use for ceremonial duties. Second was the SSVT, the Verfügungstruppen or Special Purpose Troops, and lastly the infamous Totenkopfverbände, the Death's Head Units. These latter were formed to guard Nazi Germany's burgeoning concentration camp network and were noted for their brutality and fanaticism. The Waffen-SS was promoted by Himmler as a new German imperial guard to attract ex-regular army soldiers, and the SSVT in particular saw an influx of extremely capable officers who would transform the essentially paramilitary outfits the SS were, into the first-class fighting formations envisioned by Himmler. This was the situation that was half-feared, yet half-hoped for, by their ultimate creator and father, Adolf Hitler. This influx of ex-regular army men who joined the black band were given the power to institute a series of reforms that established a military infrastructure that still has echoes in the professional armies of today.

Names to remember

But the story of Charlemagne is more than the story of political extremism and anti-communism in France, or the creation and growth of the SS; it is at heart a story of thousands of individual Frenchmen who made a conscious decision to become members of Hitler's black guards. Charlemagne's history does not begin in the early years of the war when the Waffen-SS was still an unknown and minor part of the huge and mighty Greater German Wehrmacht. In 1940 for example, there were over 10,000,000 German men aged between 18 and 34, of whom more than 6,600,000 were in the Wehrmacht, and only a tiny 50,000 were in the Waffen-SS. At that stage of the war, atrocities such as those at Le Paradis and Wormhoudt carried out by the Leibstandarte and the Totenkopf were still rare occurrences and could be viewed as aberrations, but by late 1944 when Charlemagne was being established the curtain was fast descending on the Nazi Empire and the name of the Waffen-SS would now be forever linked to the barbarities of the Eastern Front. Yet men still flocked to join; one French volunteer said of his decision to enlist:

> In 1940 the German soldiers filled me with admiration and horror. In 1943 they began to inspire pity in me. I knew that they were facing the entire world and I had a feeling that they were going to be defeated.
>
> After Stalingrad and El Alamein, we hardly ever saw any more tall, blond athletes. In the streets of Paris, I passed pale 17 or 18 year old adolescents with helmets too large for them and Mausers of the other war. Sometimes also old men with sad eyes ...

But suddenly reappeared small groups of soldiers true to the legend. Tall, silent, solitary, with both hardened and childish features. They returned from hell and the Devil was their only friend. On their collar the two 'flashes of lightning' of the Waffen-SS.[2]

So who were these volunteers and what was their story before Charlemagne?

Henri Joseph Fenet did not look the classic image of the Waffen-SS man. Of medium height he had a serious, bookish air, accentuated by the round rimmed spectacles he always wore. He was an intense young man not given to overt displays of emotion. Born on 11 July 1919, in Ceyzeriat in the Department of Ain, into a middle-class family, Fenet had no major political involvement prior to the outbreak of World War II, and was in fact a 20-year-old student preparing to become a teacher. His pre-war life was entirely unremarkable; that would change with the coming of war as he rushed to join up and defend his country.

Pierre Rostaing, on the other hand, was anything but unremarkable in the first place. Rostaing was not a patriotic citizen soldier like Fenet, volunteering when war came calling, but a professional career soldier. France has always produced such men, more comfortable in the rigours of combat than in civilian life, and this empathy with the battlefield was Rostaing's defining characteristic. He looked every inch the combat soldier, in that he was tall, strong and with a definite air of self-confidence. He was born on 8 January 1909, in Gavet in the Department of L'Isere into a working class family, and he enlisted in the French Imperial Army aged 18. Like so many of his comrades at the time he served abroad in France's vast overseas Empire, completing postings in Indochina, Morocco, Algeria and Tunisia in the twelve years he served in the army prior to 1939.

On the outbreak of the so-called Winter War in 1939, when Soviet Russia invaded tiny Finland, Rostaing was genuinely appalled by the communist invasion and saw in it the first act in an eventual Bolshevik assault on all Europe. The 2e bureau de l'Armée, French military intelligence, accepted him as a volunteer to go to Finland as a 'technical advisor'. This then was a forerunner of things to come as the Frenchman found himself fighting with the superbly trained and motivated Finnish forces against a Soviet enemy that vastly outnumbered them in both men and material on a battlefield of snow and ice. For Rostaing his battle with the Red Army would go on for almost the next seven years.

André Bayle was neither an aspiring teacher like Fenet, nor a professional warrior like Rostaing, but rather a carefree schoolboy. A strapping lad, Bayle's interest in Nazi Germany had begun when he had accompanied the French team to the Berlin Olympic Games in August 1936. The event left its mark on the young French boy who was hugely impressed by what he saw in Germany. This was his first view of the SS, when he saw members of the Leibstandarte:

> These soldiers, dressed in black, were impressive with their uniforms, their discipline, their demeanour, and their impeccable drill. Before Hitler arrived at the start of the competition, they seemed to appear from nowhere and announced Hitler's arrival, they were generously applauded by the entire stadium, by complete strangers.

To Bayle, the SS and Germany were an organisation and a country united in purpose and strength with nothing of the chaos and disorder he saw every day back in France. These then were the men who would fill the ranks of Charlemagne, but in the summer of 1939 only Rostaing wore a uniform. Then the world changed for all of them forever.

Notes

1. Edward Crankshaw, *GESTAPO Instrument of Tyranny*, Wren's Park Publishing, 2002.
2. R Forbes, *Pour L'Europe. French Volunteers in the Waffen-SS*, self-published 2000.

CHAPTER III

1940: Blitzkrieg and French Collapse

On 1 September 1939 Hitler's troops invaded Poland. Appeasement was finally seen as the chimera it was, and the Western Allies now faced war with a resurgent Nazi Germany.

The popular myth today is that while Germany's military might was a sea of armoured vehicles and screaming Stukas, the forces available to France and Britain were both small and technologically outdated. What tanks the Allies had were the World War II equivalent of lawnmowers in comparison to the massive, mechanically advanced juggernauts that equipped the multitude of Nazi panzer divisions. The truth was almost exactly the opposite. The largest standing army by number in Europe was actually France's, and supplemented by the British Expeditionary Force (BEF), let alone the as yet uncommitted Belgian and Dutch armies, the Allies actually far outnumbered the Germans in terms of men under arms. This numerical superiority was mirrored in equipment terms too, with France alone having more tanks than Nazi Germany. Many of these were obsolete but even so the mismatched contest being played out that autumn in the East with Polish cavalry charging German armour was not set for a repetition in the West.

France was a military giant and had the huge resources of her overseas Empire to call on as well. However with the vast bulk of Germany's armed forces busy subjugating Poland, including crucially all of Germany's mechanised and armoured formations, the French behemoth was struck by political and military paralysis. The opportunity for a quick, daring thrust through Germany's ill-protected western border and into the industrial heartland of the Ruhr to end the infant war at a stroke was squandered. A looming air of defeatism swept over the French political and military establishments and the result was a vacuum of political will to face Germany, and a damning lack of preparedness on the part of the much vaunted French Army. As a direct result of the mass slaughter of the trenches in World War I, French military thinking stopped at the huge fortifications of André Maginot's brainchild, the defensive wall named in his honour, the supposedly impregnable Maginot Line. However, French belief in the security afforded by the Maginot Line was to be proven as illusory as French insistence, at the beginning of the previous World War, that bayonets could overcome Maxim guns. Indeed France always seemed to be ready to fight the last war as the next one broke out, and the result was catastrophe.

Assault at Sedan

Unexpectedly for all after the Phoney War, the storm in the West broke, not over France and the Low Countries, but over Scandinavia first, Denmark and Norway falling to lightning invasions by the Nazis. With his northern flank and Swedish iron ore imports secure, Hitler launched Case Yellow (*Fall Gelb*), the invasion of France and the Low Countries, in May 1940, with Erich von Manstein's daring surprise attack through the heavily wooded Ardennes, and over the Meuse at Sedan. Caught totally unawares, the Western Allies scrambled to react, but it was all too little too late. When the advance units of German armour reached the sea at Abbeville, the campaign was effectively over as a contest. Cut in two the Allied armies desperately sought to regain the initiative but to no avail. In the northern pocket the majority of the BEF, with assorted French and Belgian allies, was hemmed in with its back to the sea. Only the miracle of Operation Dynamo saved enough out of the carnage at Dunkirk to give Britain a chance of defending herself from the seemingly inevitable German invasion.

South of the German breakthrough at Abbeville, the majority of the hitherto much feared French Army was pushed back behind the Somme river, where along with some BEF units, including the superb 51st Highland Division, they were battered into retreat and submission. The French units facing Mussolini's Fascist Italy across the Alps, including elite Chasseurs Alpins units, heroically stood their ground when the Italian dictator tried to get in on the act by invading France in her death throes. However, as the mauled Italian units retreated in panic from determined and skilful French resistance, German forces flooded southwards crushing all who stood in their way. Seemingly unable to mount an effective defence, the French Army was carved up by coordinated German assaults and ground into pieces. Organised resistance collapsed and the rest of France fell in a matter of weeks. Hundreds of thousands of Frenchmen surrendered en masse and marched into Nazi captivity, along with many units of colonial soldiers of whom some were shot out of hand by German soldiers in a foretaste of the racial war that was to come in the East. The fall of France was a military and political earthquake. The nation at the head of the second largest empire in the world, victor of the trenches twenty years earlier, and possessor of the most powerful armed forces in Europe, had been conquered in a short summer campaign.

Darnard's war

Like so many of his fellow countrymen Darnard, immediately on hearing of the declaration of war, abandoned his previous anti-government political agitation and rushed to join the colours to defend *'la belle France'*. All animosity was forgotten in a wave of patriotism that swept the country and the recruiting offices were filled to overflowing. Darnard volunteered for service, and was accepted back into uniform. However, much to his disgust he was assigned to an administrative role rather than a combat one due to his age – he was 42 years old. Undaunted Darnard repeatedly applied for frontline duty, and eventually his ceaseless badgering was rewarded and his request was granted. Indeed his own recommendation as to his role was also accepted and he was tasked to set up raiding units within his division modelled on those he had formed and led in World War I.

Darnard used the time afforded by the Phoney War well in recruiting and training his raiding units, and with the beginning of hostilities proper he led his men in some hard combat along the Maginot Line. During the fighting he was again decorated for bravery as in the First World War but was then finally captured by the Germans in June 1940 and imprisoned. Following the Armistice and the establishment of the Vichy French regime he escaped and fled southwards out of the northern occupation zone and back to Nice.

This was the turning point for Darnard. Like so many of his fellow countrymen he was shocked, appalled and disgusted by the ease of the German conquest. By now a decorated veteran of both World Wars, he looked around for the reasons his beloved France had failed to stand up to the Blitzkrieg, and found them in the supposed 'enemies of the state' he had faced prior to the outbreak of war; the communists, socialists and the political Left in general. Darnard resolved to destroy those whom he now saw as parasites and traitors and resurrect the honour of France. He threw himself into nationalist politics, but at this stage he was overtly hostile to the Germans whom he regarded as the cursed invaders and despoilers of his beloved country.

German triumph, French disbelief – Vichy France

The joy of victory in Germany was matched by the sheer disbelief in France itself. French public confidence in the establishment, already weak prior to the invasion, was shattered completely. Suffering a crisis of self-confidence, riven with internal dissent and embittered by years of political conflict between Right and Left, the political emergence of the elderly Marshal Philippe Pétain, the hero of Verdun, seemed to offer a stunned French populace a way of re-establishing some sense of order from the chaos.

Pétain's own brand of paternalism founded on a rallying cry of 'country, family, religion' gave the people a moral foundation many feared they had lost, and allowed the French an illusion of independence with the creation of the Unoccupied Zone under the control of the new Government at Vichy. The victor of Verdun brought a sense of security and leadership to a nation sorely in need of both. At first the faith placed in him by the people seemed to be vindicated with the deal reached in the terms of the armistice signed at Compiègne on 24 June 1940 in the same railway carriage in which Germany had suffered a similar humiliation over twenty years earlier. Pétain seemed to have come to some sort of accommodation with the Germans; yes France was beaten but a large part of her metropolitan territory was to be free of occupation and ruled by a French government from Vichy. Her Empire was safe, and Germany seemed to look upon her as a possible partner in a new European order, rather than as a conquered foe. Over time this was to be proven a complete and utter falsehood. Like so many others Darnard believed Pétain was the only hope of resurrecting French glory and he became a fervent Pétainist and supporter of Vichy.

De Gaulle and the Free French
At this time resistance to the Germans by the Free French under de Gaulle was nothing more than a footnote. De Gaulle was a little-known and obscure French Army officer whose name was familiar to no one other than a small circle of military experts in the field of modern armoured warfare. This niche position in the military world could not compare to the near legendary status of Philippe Pétain, the heroic Victor of Verdun. True, de Gaulle had led his armoured formations well in the otherwise disastrous 1940 summer campaign, and he was determined to fight on, but in reality the Free French forces were weak, curiously mostly based on Foreign Legion units, with no heavy equipment and little presence in the all-important French Empire. Indeed not only did most Frenchmen not recognise de Gaulle and his forces as legitimate representatives of France, many of them believed that they had actually abandoned France by escaping to England, and that they should have stayed and defended the homeland instead. This widely held popular view was reinforced by subsequent events during the initial occupation.

German troops garrisoned in France were under strict orders to treat the local population respectfully and with courtesy. Assaults on French civilians and seizure of property were forbidden and transgressors were treated harshly, and while fraternisation with French women was not officially encouraged (as it was in 'Aryan' countries such as Norway and Denmark), it was not discouraged either. At a time when over 2,000,000 young Frenchmen were in German POW camps, events took a predictably human turn and relations between occupied and occupier eased.

In this tense, but not hostile, atmosphere acts of active resistance were few. Popular cries to continue the fight against the Germans were muted and were quietened further when the Royal Navy sank the French fleet at anchor in Mers-el-Kebir near Oran in Algeria to ensure it didn't fall into German hands. This act and the loss of hundreds of French lives it entailed convinced many that France's future lay not with its ancient enemy over the Channel but with the New European Order envisioned by Hitler and increasingly extolled by his Minister for Propaganda, Joseph Goebbels. When this was articulated under the banner of an anti-bolshevik crusade it chimed well with the basic tenets of the French political and philosophical right wing, and many Frenchmen were increasingly drawn from a stance of neutrality to one of active collaboration with the Nazis.

French collaboration

To brand all those Frenchmen who fought with the Germans simply as traitors to France, is to grossly oversimplify a complex issue. After conquering France the Nazis did not place the entire country under direct military rule but allowed the French to install Pétain and his government as the legal and legitimate government of France at the time. Therefore, on a technical level, de Gaulle and his forces were subject to Pétain and by establishing himself in opposition to Vichy, de Gaulle was acting against the authority of his legally constituted national government. This legal argument, of course, needs to be viewed in context and the greater need to combat Hitler, however, at a time when so many of the old pre-war certainties had disappeared in the maelstrom of defeat, the issues of legality and legitimacy were important and for many Frenchmen and women gave them clear guidance as to where their loyalties should lie; for most at least initially this was with Pétain and his policies of collaboration with the Germans.

To demonstrate the complexity of the confusion that many ordinary people in France then had to face, consider the position of the populations of Alsace-Lorraine. These beautiful provinces of steeply wooded hills and ancient towns and cities, such as Metz and Strasbourg, had long been the meeting place between French and Germanic cultures and peoples. The region that boasted the birthplace of that most famous of all French heroines, Joan of Arc, was also the second home of Germanic wine and beer production and where a man's neighbour was just as likely to be called Schmidt as Duvall. The provinces formed part of France prior to

Germany's unification in the 19th century, before being annexed by a victorious Prussia after the Franco-Prussian War in 1871. Lost to Germany and reunited with France post the Versailles Treaty at the end of World War I, the 1940 Armistice saw them rejoin Germany after a twenty-one year interlude. As such the male population became liable for conscription in the Wehrmacht and to all intents and purposes were treated no differently from other Germans in provinces such as Saxony, Thuringia or Hesse. Such was the confusion of the situation that a young man might well have been born a Frenchman to German parents, the father having served in the Imperial German Army and the grandfather in the French Imperial Army, and then found himself called up for service in the Wehrmacht, only to be told he was a Frenchman again at the end of the war while being in a POW camp in German uniform. This may seem far fetched but at the end of the war a number of Alsatians were brought to trial for the horrific Oradour-sur-Glane massacre committed while they were serving in the Der Führer regiment of the 2nd SS Panzer Division Das Reich. At the time of their trials they were legally Frenchmen and there was a significant and popular campaign in Alsace-Lorraine that stressed the ambiguity of their previous positions and highlighted the need for the country to move on and heal itself. The trials were ruinous for a France struggling to come to terms with the war, and when finally convicted the sentences passed on the ex-Waffen-SS grenadiers were either commuted or quietly dropped by a French Government struggling to paper over the cracks exposed by four years of occupation, collaboration, resistance and bloodshed.

In these desperate and morally tortuous circumstances an Alsatian serving with de Gaulle could legally be tried for treason by Vichy if captured. In such a situation the issue of treason then becomes less of a legal question and becomes one of morality, belief and perception.

After France's defeat it is undeniable that a large part of French society put their faith in Pétain and Vichy to deliver them from despair. Pétain's call for an end to democracy and a return to the values of 'country, order and family' was well received. French society craved stability after so many years of turbulence, and Vichy seemed to be the answer. For many Frenchmen and women, particularly the young, the contrast between their own military defeat and the political and moral vacuum that had fuelled it, was in stark contrast to the power and purpose of Nazi Germany.

The Service d'Ordre Légionnaire, the Milice française and French civil war

Darnard built up his power and influence in Vichy until in July 1941 he founded the Service d'Ordre Légionnaire (SOL), an unofficial volunteer paramilitary organisation whose role was envisioned by Darnard to support the official forces of Vichy law and order against any and all internal enemies and to act as a popular bulwark of support for Pétain. At first the SOL was manifestly popular, as testified to by French citizens:

> The Legion was very popular and when Pétain visited Marseille the enthusiasm was enormous. People at first believed that the Germans were protecting them against the Bolsheviks. And there was a lot of Anglophobia, members of the Legion made continuous speeches against Russia and against England.[1]

The uniformed but unarmed SOL members did little more than attend rallies and processions, but by wearing the uniform itself they openly identified themselves as Pétainists to members of the fledgling underground Resistance, both Free French Gaullist, and communists following the German invasion of the Soviet Union on 22 June 1941. Several SOL members were subsequently murdered by these early *résistants*, but barring a decision by Vichy to supply them with arms there was little the Legion could do to protect its members. Then in January 1943 the decision was made by Darnard to change the SOL's name to the now-infamous Milice française. This change in title coincided with an upturn in the campaign of assassinations against it as a standard bearer of support for Pétain and Vichy. This had nothing to do with the change of name, but rather was a sign of increased organisation and militancy on the part of the *résistants*. The Milice itself was still unarmed and therefore its members were just as soft targets as they were before. The change from the SOL to the Milice did nothing initially to protect its members and dozens of newly named Miliciens were murdered by the various Resistance factions throughout the Vichy zone during 1943. Between April and the end of November 1943, for example, a total of thirty-three Miliciens were killed and a further twenty-five seriously wounded in Resistance attacks.

Not surprisingly the pressure on Vichy was intense from both the Miliciens and from Darnard himself to arm the organisation to at least allow a measure of self-defence, though the idea of using them to actively fight the emerging Resistance networks directly was also starting to feature in German and extreme right-wing French thinking. In this way the activities of the Resistance actually played a part in helping to drive the Milice down the road of armed collaboration with the Germans. What had started as an anti-communist, but also a nationalist anti-German, movement was now moving inexorably into alliance with the Nazis. Facing the real dangers posed by an armed Resistance the Milice turned to the only people who could supply them with the means to fight back, the German Wehrmacht. In what was increasingly resembling a French civil war the Milice were now aligning themselves with the German occupiers, albeit uneasily. This conflict between strident French nationalism on the one hand and the neces-sity of collaboration with the Germans on the other was the conundrum at the heart of the Milice and would be replicated in Charlemagne when ex-Miliciens exported their problems to the fledgling formation.

Throughout this period, from France's surrender in 1940 to D-Day in 1944, Pétain remained detached and aloof from the machinations of the Right, unable and unwilling to reconcile the growing contradictions at the heart of his administration. How could a much avowed French nationalism co-exist with an acceptance of German conquerors sitting in Paris? Pétain was finding that by doing the deal with Hitler that Churchill refused to, that is retention of the overseas Empire (in this case the French one) in exchange for acceptance of German hegemony in Europe, he was supping from a poisoned chalice. However, by this stage in the war it was too late to turn back and for many in France itself the view was that to be Pétainist was to be in alliance with the Nazis. Pétain himself still refused to see this and kept a distance from political figures he viewed as overtly collaborationist or too pro-Nazi.

Darnard, Doriot and Déat were the most notable of these 'untouchables'. But this situation could not go on indefinitely, and finally, in December 1943 Darnard was at last brought into the Vichy Government on Hitler's insistence, becoming the Secretary-General for the Maintenance of Order and Head of Police in Vichy. Déat was also meant to be included but Pétain resisted and won that minor concession from the Germans. This was fol-lowed in January 1944 by Darnard being formally installed as the Minister of the Interior for Vichy France. During this time Darnard's Milice enjoyed an almost official status that saw their numbers swell to over 35,000 by the beginning of 1944, though most were either active in name only or not suitable for combat duty. Of the entire organisation fewer than 5,000 were both willing and able to engage the Resistance in open combat, and these men were placed in special *franc-garde* units and made available for anti-partisan operations, though the vexed question of their relationship with the Germans was still unresolved. *Franc-garde* units did then engage the *résistants*, and even conducted a series of anti-partisan sweeps through areas of heavy Resistance activity, but they were unable to do this alone due to lack of armaments, organisation and numbers, and inevitably there was heavy reliance on the active cooperation of the Wehrmacht in order to ensure any sort of operational success.

Anti-bolshevik crusade
For many Frenchmen collaboration did not mean they were adherents of the Nazi cause, but rather they saw in its virtues the rebirth of a new and resurgent France. France has always had an obsession with its place

in Europe and the world, and that place for most Frenchmen and women is at the forefront. The Gallic temperament is one which does not favour standing in anyone's shadow or leaving any slight, real or imagined, unanswered. The trumpets of Austerlitz, Wagram and the glory days of the Napoleonic era can still be heard in the French soul and from that springs the absolute French need for *'la gloire'*. For the French it was obvious that their nation with its history, traditions, culture and Empire, should be a leading world power again. The result was that for many Frenchmen cooperation with the Nazis was not seen or accepted as treason but a means to an end, and a strongly nationalist end at that with a virile, powerful France reborn as they believed Germany had been. Vichy propounded this theory and gave it bureaucratic legitimacy; it was called state collaboration – *'collaboration d'Etat'*.

This was pragmatism, with political and economic cooperation with Nazi Germany in order to safeguard French interests and ensure France obtained a powerful and influential position in a German-dominated Europe. The state adopted features common in Nazi Germany as part of its drive for rejuvenation. Large-scale, patriotic, nationalistic organisations flourished under Pétain. The taking up of arms to combat the enemies of the French people and French culture was applauded and supported. This was particularly focused on the struggle against Bolshevism and France's deep rift between the ideologies of the far Right and Left. Communism as a force in French society was only matched in its strength by anti-communism. One French household would celebrate the short-lived life of the Paris Commune of 1871, while its neighbour would rejoice in its oppression and fear its possible return. Such passions were held in check by the Nazis as long as the 1939 Nazi-Soviet Non-Aggression Pact remained in force, but on 22 June 1941, with the opening of Operation Barbarossa and Nazi Germany's attempt to conquer the Soviet Union, those passions were fuelled by the Nazi call for a European-wide anti-bolshevik crusade to save Europe from the menace to the East. This call chimed with Vichy propaganda and the strong tradition of anti-bolshevism in much of French society.

The next step of combining with the Nazis to fight these supposed enemies was no longer such a leap away. This was the road that led many young Frenchmen from service with the French Army in 1939–40, to membership of a Pétainist paramilitary organisation and finally on to active collaboration with the Nazis. This then was personal collaboration – *'le collaborationisme'* – an ideologically motivated cooperation with the Nazis that was mostly founded on preventing the spread of Bolshevism.

On the German side there were some high profile Francophiles such as the Foreign Minister, Joachim von Ribbentrop, and the German ambassador to Vichy, Otto Abetz, but for most Nazis France was seen as a useful economic resource to be exploited for the benefit of the Fatherland.

This was in particular the view of Reichsmarschall Hermann Goering, head of the Luftwaffe and architect of Germany's economic Four Year Plans. Goering and others in the Nazi hierarchy did not view France as an equal in the new European order, but as a conquered nation peopled by an inferior race of non-Aryans. As such France was a source of labour and agricultural and industrial produce, but not a partner in the struggle against Bolshevism.

With this as the prevailing Nazi view, France was plundered for workers. It is estimated that eight to nine million Frenchmen and women worked directly for the Germans on roads, military defences, aircraft, armaments and food production. Compulsion was used to extract benefit for the Reich but was not always needed. For example, in 1941 the French photographic company, Photomaton, offered to produce identity photos for Jews in Nazi concentration camps with no prompting from the Nazi authorities at all; it was seen as a business opportunity. However, as German fortunes in the war worsened and the drain on resources for the Eastern Front grew inexorably, there was a need for more workers than could be supplied by volunteering alone. The result was the introduction of compulsory forced labour, *Service du travail obligatoire* (STO), introduced at German insistence in February 1943. Faced with this compulsion many young Frenchmen opted to 'go to the maquis' and swell the ranks of the Resistance, but many did not and over 650,000 men and 44,000 women ended up going to Germany before the end of the war as labourers. This huge migration was second only behind Poland in terms of the numbers of unskilled workers sent to the Reich, and first in the number of skilled workers conscripted. That astonishing fact should be remembered too in terms of the difference in the level of compulsion used by the Nazis in Poland as against their far gentler methods in France.

Names to remember

When the war came Henri Fenet was a student at the Paris University of Henri IV studying for the entrance exam for Paris's premier teacher training college, the Ecole normale Supérieure, and as with so many idealistic students of whatever nationality Fenet was caught up in the mood of patriotism that swept the nation, and immediately enlisted. He was selected to attend the Ecole spéciale militaire of Saint-Cyr, France's equivalent of Britain's famed Royal Military Academy Sandhurst, and was then commissioned Aspirant (officer cadet) and posted to the anti-tank company of the 3e division d'infanterie coloniale. When the Germans invaded in May 1940 Fenet and his unit were involved in bitter fighting with the advancing Wehrmacht during which time he was twice wounded in combat and awarded the Croix de Guerre for his bravery under fire.

Then came the collapse and ignominious defeat. Fenet was shattered, and like so many of his fellow servicemen he then faced a decision about his personal response to the calamity. Rejecting the idea of leaving for England and joining de Gaulle, Fenet returned to the Vichy Zone and joined the newly established 100,000-strong Vichy Armistice Army as an infantry Aspirant and was posted to Mauritania in French central Africa where he commanded a platoon of Senegalese *tirailleurs*. On the completion of a successful tour his next posting was to attend the Ecole militaire d'infanterie of Saint-Maixent, temporarily relocated to Aix-en-Provence, for further training. He was still undergoing training there in November 1942 when Operation Torch, the Allied invasion of French North Africa, was launched. The German response was the invasion of the unoccupied Zone of metropolitan France as they lost faith in Vichy's reliability as an ally. With total occupation the Armistice Army was disbanded and Fenet was demobilised on 29 November 1942 with the rank of sous-lieutenant (second lieutenant).

In less than three years Henri Fenet had witnessed the disintegration of not one but two French national armies and for a patriot it was indeed a bitter pill to swallow. He returned home to Ceyzeriat with no clear plan of what to do next, but whilst there his father suggested he attend a meeting with the local SOL chief, a retired Army major. Unenthusiastic but with little else to do Fenet met the man and listened as he was told that one day he would be needed in a new French Army, and that in the meantime he could not sit idle but must prepare for that day. As a result he joined the Pétainist SOL, and then the Milice française on its inauguration in January 1943. He rose quickly through the ranks and was soon appointed the Head of the Milice in the department of Ain. But for Fenet the Milice was just a staging post; he now saw France's national humiliation in the context of a communist threat against the whole continent, and the organisation calling out to all of Europe's youth to join together in defence of their collective European identity was the Waffen-SS. On 18 October 1943, at the age of 24, Henri Joseph Fenet enlisted in the Waffen-SS.

Germany's blitzkrieg against the West found Pierre Rostaing returned from his stint in Finland and serving in metropolitan France. He fought against the invading Germans with his customary professionalism, but found himself, as in Finland, on the losing side yet again. Like Fenet he then joined the Vichy Armistice Army. Still concerned at what he perceived as the growing communist threat, on 13 October 1942 Rostaing joined the Pétainist Légion Tricolore, intended as an official successor armed force to the initially unofficial LVF. But the Nazis were not comfortable with the creation of an overtly nationalist Vichy military organisation that could, as they saw it, challenge their hegemony. On Hitler's orders the Germans disbanded the Legion. Rostaing was now out of uniform for the first time in his adult life, his reaction was immediate, and he enlisted in the LVF.

André Bayle spent the years of invasion, collapse and Vichy government chaffing to get in on the action but he was still a schoolboy, being only 13 years old when World War II broke out. But on 15 March 1943, only just aged 16, he boldly entered the recruiting office and volunteered for the Waffen-SS. On being accepted he was initially sent to Clignancourt Barracks in Paris, and then on to the training camp with all the other French SS volunteers at Sennheim in Alsace-Lorraine.

Note

1. Oral testimony from Madeleine Baudoin, member of the French Resistance (Marseille, 6 September 1971), in H R Kedward, *Resistance in Vichy France*, Oxford University Press, 1978.

CHAPTER IV

The Waffen-SS and Foreign Recruitment

The situation in France, both in the Occupied and Unoccupied Zones, seemed ripe for exploitation by the Nazis for their own military ends, but who among the plethora of competing military and paramilitary organisations would take advantage? This might seem an odd question, but the German military was not the picture of efficiency that is the commonly held perception of the public, but rather it was a host of different services and organisations riven by petty jealousies and feuding that more often than not concentrated their energies on one-upmanship within the Nazi German state than focusing on purely winning the war against external foes. In this the German military exactly mirrored the organisation of the Nazi state itself, where Hitler encouraged internal competition to safeguard his own ultimate power. So would the Heer, the Kriegsmarine, the Luftwaffe be first off the mark, or would it be someone else? At first the fastest proved to be the German Army, the Heer, closely followed by the Kriegsmarine, but waiting in the wings was Nazi Germany's other army, the Waffen-SS.

Hausser and Steiner – architects of the Waffen-SS

Paul Hausser, a retired German Army general, and Felix Steiner, an advocate of the elite stormtrooper ethos, were both veterans of the carnage of World War I. They held similar views as to the utter wastefulness of the tactics of those huge World War I infantry armies and both were determined that there was a better way. Together, though the relationship was often strained between the Prussian general Hausser and the trench tough Steiner, they devised a military system for the Waffen-SS that was nothing short of a revolution in its day. The ethos and systems they embedded would transform a minor patchwork of paramilitary units into a pre-eminent military machine that would draw parallels with warrior castes throughout the ages such as the Spartans, the Roman Praetorians and the Byzantine Varangian Guard, and it would accomplish this in the ridiculously short time span of little more than a decade!

The Waffen-SS training that Hausser and Steiner inaugurated was founded on one overriding principle: the unvarnished pursuit of excellence in every aspect of the profession of arms. Service in the Waffen-SS was not portrayed in the Christian tradition of a staid homage to a sad but unfortunately necessary duty, but rather it harked back unashamedly to a pagan heartfelt celebration of the pure joy of combat. In this view war was not something to be avoided if at all possible, but an act to be celebrated, and to excel in war was the ultimate accolade for any individual or nation. This mantra, complete anathema to the European Christian tradition of the belief in the evils of war, was the foundation upon which the Waffen-SS was built. SS troopers were trained to enjoy battle for its own sake, to lust after it, to forsake feelings of pity and remorse and thrill in the violence of it all. These emotions harked back to the warrior traditions of earlier times and were reinforced by the heavy use of symbolism so prevalent in military culture. The use of the pagan *sig* runes, as the symbol of their allegiance and to distinguish the entire organisation, was a nod to that violent past. The Waffen-SS had a name for the quality they sought and celebrated, they called it '*Härte*'. This meant many things, including toughness in battle, fearlessness, ruthlessness in the execution of orders and dedication to victory at all costs. It also meant contempt for the enemy and for death, and brutality to all who stood in their way. The Waffen-SS viewed themselves not just as soldiers, but fighters, who engaged in combat for its own sake. An American officer, who fought against the Leibstandarte in the Ardennes in 1944 reported the following:

> These men revealed a form of fighting that is new to me. They are obviously soldiers, but they fight as if military ways were of no consequence. They actually seem to enjoy combat.

An SS-Haupsturmführer, a Captain, recalled the 'sheer beauty' of the fighting in Russia in 1942, stating:

> it was well worth the dreadful suffering, after a time we got to the point where we were concerned not for ourselves, or even Germany, but lived entirely for the next clash.

This then was *Härte*. In this pursuit of martial excellence, the hallmarks were innovation, unconventionality and a willingness to experiment. This was entirely different from regular German Army training which was dominated by the tried and tested methods of Prussian tradition. For instance, whereas the regular army used parade ground close-order drill to instil discipline and teamwork into new recruits, in the Waffen-SS square bashing played only a minor part, and was actually abolished completely in 1942.

Waffen-SS training

For a Waffen-SS recruit basic training lasted an initial gruelling three weeks, and was based on the three pillars of physical fitness, character development and weapons training.

Achieving and maintaining a peak of physical fitness was a prerequisite for soldiers of the Waffen-SS, and the key was through sports, particularly team ones in which all ranks competed together. Waffen-SS sporting facilities were first class and were utilised to encourage camaraderie and promote extremely high levels of physical fitness and endurance. For example, Steiner's troops could cover three kilometres in full kit in twenty minutes; such a thing was unheard of in the Army. Echoes of this policy of the value of sports in military training can be seen in most modern professional armies of today, indeed the weekly 'sports afternoon' in the British Army is often the highlight of the training week, and participation of officers and men together is heavily promoted.

In terms of character development, aggression, initiative and self-reliance were encouraged. This was not only for other ranks, but also for officers and those aspiring to be officers. This all-ranks emphasis was a distinguishing feature of the Waffen-SS. To become an officer an individual first became an officer-candidate and served in the ranks, getting to know his future soldiers and earning their respect. And while rigid demarcations of class reinforced the divide between officers and men in the Army, in the Waffen-SS the standard form of address was '*Kamerad*' when off-duty, with all ranks eating together in joint officer/other ranks messes. Privates and NCOs saw that their officers earned their rank and promotion on merit, and not on social class and education, with the result that there was an extraordinary closeness between Waffen-SS officers and their soldiers. The far higher proportion of officer-candidates from non-traditional military families in the Waffen-SS, as opposed to the Army, made this process easier, and its value was proved again and again on battlefields across a continent.

In March 1942 a secret report by the Nazi's own intelligence service, the Sicherheitsdienst (SD), commented on the German public's perception of the Waffen-SS:

> by its achievements the Waffen-SS has won its place in the popular esteem. Particular reference is made to the good comradeship between officers, NCOs and men.

This fundamental bond of trust and mutual respect with other Waffen-SS men was continually reinforced in training throughout every aspect of a recruit's life. For example, every recruit had a locker, which as all soldiers know is home to an individual's personal possessions and their only refuge of privacy throughout their training. But in the Waffen-SS recruits were forbidden to lock their lockers as a demonstration of trust in their fellows. To break that trust was therefore to strike at a central Waffen-SS value and was penalised with the utmost harshness. An apocryphal tale is told by SS veterans that two recruits were caught stealing from a comrade's locker, they were tried, convicted and sentenced to death for the offence. After being shot in front of their comrades they were buried in an unmarked grave that was then marched over by their entire unit as a sign of their contempt. Whether true or not it is a fact that stealing was a very rare offence among Waffen-SS recruits!

Familiarity and mastery of all battlefield weapons was the third pillar in a recruit's initial training. Live firing exercises are a standard part of any modern army's training syllabus, and have been for decades. However the Waffen-SS were the first force to systematically institute the practice and use of live firing exercises in training, and take them seriously. Large amounts of training time were spent on realistic, and multiple, live firing scenarios in which casualties, and even fatalities, were sustained. The oft heard retort from Waffen-SS commanders to Army dismay over such casualties, was that every drop of blood spilled in peacetime would save a river in war. Marksmanship skills were also highly prized; winning battles required soldiers to hit their targets and the rapid and accurate application of firepower was an essential skill.

Time was also spent on night manoeuvres, field craft and camouflage techniques. The Waffen-SS famously adopted camouflage pattern uniforms to replace the ubiquitous German field grey, a decision for which they were ridiculed at the time, but is now standard across the armies of the world. The reality is that Felix Steiner, or indeed any graduate of the Waffen-SS training regime, would recognise most aspects of the training schedules of any modern professional army with their emphasis on combat techniques, particularly for the night-time battlefield, rather than old fashioned spit, polish and drill.

This Waffen-SS hunger for differentiation from the Army and love of everything modern extended to battlefield doctrine. The widely-held popular view of the German Army that began World War II was that it consisted of an endless wave of tanks and armoured vehicles supported by armadas of aircraft, the classic view of Blitzkrieg. The reality was that the vast majority of the German Army in 1939 was either on foot or horse-drawn, and this remained true for almost the entire war. This could also have been true for the Waffen-SS, but from the first the emphasis in training for the black guards was on an all-arms battle where the key to victory was aggression, decisive shock action and all-arms fighting together as a whole. This doctrine would dominate Waffen-SS military thinking and consequent actions throughout the war.

The recruits

In terms of who volunteered for such a force the recruitment standards went through several definite stages during the course of the history of the organisation. Initially at least the Waffen-SS was the epitome of Himmler's racial fantasy of an Aryan physical elite. Pre-war recruits were expected to be already well-versed in Nazi ideology, and as stated in *Der Soldatenfreund* :

Every pure-blooded German in good health [can] become a member. He must be of excellent character, have no criminal record, and be an ardent adherent to all National Socialist doctrines. Members of the Streifendienst and of the Hitler Youth will be given preference because their aptitudes and schooling are indicative that they have become acquainted with the ideology of the SS.

Recruits had to be between the ages of 17 and 22, a minimum of 168cm tall (5'9" – Himmler's height), and with no criminal record. From 1935 onwards the requirement to prove a 'pure' Aryan genealogy, dating back to 1800 for enlisted men and 1750 for officers, was instituted. Terms of service were a minimum of four years for rankers, twelve years for NCOs and twenty-five years for officers.

Indeed the requirements were so stringent that only fifteen out of every 100 applicants were finally accepted. Himmler himself boasted that he personally viewed the photographs of all officer applicants for the Waffen-SS to ensure no one was accepted without exhibiting a requisite level of 'Nordic features'. There was also the oft quoted fascination with perfect dental health! The boast being that applicants were turned down even if they had a single filling. Bizarre as it seems, this hurdle of dentistry was a recurring theme among all foreign recruitment for the Wehrmacht as well. For example, on 28 August 1941, during the recruitment for the Army-sponsored French Légion des Volontaires Français contre le bolchevisme (LVF), German doctors examined 1,679 volunteers and rejected some 800, of which the majority were for bad teeth! These fantasist extremes did not go down well with many of the more practical SS leaders, including Sepp Dietrich of the Leibstandarte, particularly as the war progressed, casualties mounted and the ranks thinned.

The cradle of the European SS: Bad Tölz

In addition to their revolutionary training regime, Hausser and Steiner insisted on establishing an infrastructure that would be able to deliver their vision and produce the required end result of an outstanding military elite. First and foremost was the need to train an officer corps, and not just any officer corps, but a body of men who would epitomise the new breed of the Waffen-SS. This led to the establishment of the SS Junkerschulen (Officer Candidate Schools) of Bad Tölz and Braunschweig. These academies were centres of excellence for the profession of arms, and by 1937 were graduating over 400 officers a year, in two sets of classes. The key role played by the schools in the Waffen-SS is amply demonstrated by the fact that the majority of Knight's Crosses awarded to the Waffen-SS were made to graduates of Bad Tölz and Braunschweig.

The pupils tended not to be strategic thinkers; indeed before 1938 some 40% of entrants had received no more than elementary education, and few graduates rose to the highest military ranks. But at battalion and company level the Junkerschule graduates were formidable, if brutal, leaders. The aggressive doctrine taught at the schools was not without cost though. For example, by 1942 almost every member of the 1934–5 Bad Tölz class of sixty graduates had been killed in action. In time Bad Tölz in particular became the cradle of the Waffen-SS's transformation to become a multinational army. In 1943 it established its first class (or 'Inspection' as it was called) exclusively for west European volunteers. Previously the foreign volunteers had received no special treatment and were treated like Germans.

Within the next two years, SS Junkerschule Tölz would produce more than 1,000 highly motivated European officers from twelve different countries exclusive of Germany. The training they received was of the highest standard in some of the finest facilities available. Bad Tölz classes were treated to opera, musical and theatrical performances from the best troupes Europe could provide, and the athletics facilities were unsurpassed. Twelve different coaches, each one either an Olympic or world class champion in his field, supervised a vast sports programme that even included golf and tennis. Other Waffen-SS training establishments followed the lead of Bad Tölz, such as the SS NCO school in Klagenfurt, and it is the officer and NCO training schools that set the tone for an army, as any graduates of Sandhurst, West Point or the British Army's Platoon Sergeants Battle Course at Brecon will tell you.

Recruitment standards drop

However, as the war progressed recruitment standards were continually eroded, until by the time of the formation of Charlemagne even the most basic standards would be gone, with the Waffen-SS welcoming men of every nationality and ethnic group into their ranks, and even resorting to conscription as the fundamental tenet of the 'volunteer' gave way under the pressure of the need to supply reinforcements to the Eastern Front in particular. This abandonment of standards would see the Waffen-SS evolve in Nazi rhetoric from a racial German elite into a huge polyglot army combating bolshevism and numbering over 980,000 men under arms by the end of the war. Of this total only some 400,000 were actually Reich Germans. Many of the rest were considered suitably Aryan, according to Nazi racial theory, but many were not. In total some 137,000 West Europeans served in the Waffen-SS including 50,000 Dutchmen, 23,000 Flemings, 20,000 Italians, 15,000 Walloons, 11,000 Danes, 8,000 French, 6,000 Norwegians and 1,000 Finns.

Most of these were acceptable as Aryans, as were the 185,000 racial Germans from outside the Reich's borders, the Volksdeutsche. These racial Germans came from all over, including 80,000 from Hungary, 45,000 from Czechoslovakia, 25,000 from Croatia, around 16,000 from western Europe, 8,000 from Romania, 5,000 from Serbia, 5,000 from Poland, some 775 from Scandinavia, only 100 from the Soviet Union (proving Stalin's efficiency when he eliminated the Volga German people in 1941), a further eighty-four from France, and even a reputed five ethnic Germans from the USA! But some like the Walloons, Italians and French were not considered Aryan, and were therefore unsuitable as Waffen-SS men, at least at first. Even worse racially were the 200,000 men who served from the Ukraine, Belorussia, Russia itself, the Baltic states and the Balkans.

What didn't change as the war progressed was the Waffen-SS's allegiance to innovation in their training regimes. For example, as late as 1944 the youthful panzer crews of the 12th SS Panzer Division Hitlerjugend were required, as part of their training, to spend a week working on the assembly line at the MAN tank factory in Nürnberg. It was believed that if they were going to crew the tank it would be beneficial for them to know how it was built in the first place. Lessons learned on the battlefield were quickly adopted in the training establishments back home, with combat veterans rotated back as instructors to pass on hard won knowledge from the Front. This was often to teach about the various problems experienced in different terrains and climates and also the combat techniques of the enemy. Such throrough and comprehensive training became extremely important as the war went on, and ultimately saved the lives of many a Waffen-SS trooper.

The spur for the first major change in recruitment standards was the virulent opposition of the Army to Waffen-SS expansion. Control of Germany's manpower of military age was firmly in the hands of the Wehrmacht. As such the flow of recruits to the Waffen-SS was restricted by the suspicious authorities to a trickle, less than 2% of the national manpower pool, and Himmler was forced to look to the brutalised Totenkopf concentration camp guards and the elderly reservists of the Ordnungspolizei to swell his ranks. This was hardly the ideal of the Teutonic centurion! The successful participation by the Leibstandarte, the SSVT and Totenkopf units in the invasion of Poland led to some relaxation in the flow of recruits by the Army, especially after some judicial prodding by Hitler, but even so the Waffen-SS contribution to the success of the 1940 campaign in the West was still minor. But in his drive to expand the SS, Himmler found a willing and able lieutenant in the pugnacious Swabian SS-Gruppenführer Gottlob Berger. Berger was a tireless and talented organiser who, together with Himmler, devised a unique and revolutionary answer to the recruitment problems of the Waffen-SS. If Germany was closed to them then they would recruit from outside the borders of the Third Reich.

Berger and the Volksdeutsche

Henceforth the shortfall in recruits from Germany would be filled by two distinct and hitherto untapped reservoirs of suitable manpower – firstly 'racial' Germans living outside her national boundaries, the Volksdeutsche, and secondly out and out foreigners, the Freiwilligen. The Waffen-SS was going global!

This strangely fitted with Himmler's world vision, because alongside his love of detail, bureaucracy and intrigue, Himmler had another side, that of a crackpot fantasist. His crank philosophy was an amalgamation of mysticism, Germanic racial history and a twisted theory of genetics. Himmler's view included Hitler's all-pervading anti-Semitism and belief in a 'great racial destiny' for the German *Volk*. It also drew on the theories of the Nazi Party's so-called 'philosopher and thinker', Alfred Rosenberg. However Himmler's racial landscape went far beyond Rosenberg's illusory theories, and control of the myriad branches of the SS organisation gave Himmler the ability to turn his most weird imaginings into reality.

Expeditions were sent as far as Tibet and Japan to investigate supposed archaeological foundations for the 'Aryans' as a distinct race. Detailed scientific research was conducted into the supposed inheritance of Aryan vs Semitic facial and skeletal features, and a massive sum was spent on converting the semi-ruined Schloss Wewelsburg in central Germany into a Hollywood-esque Gothic 'home' of the SS. Himmler even 'themed' each of the guest bedrooms in the renovated castle after historic Germanic heroes, such as King Henry the Fowler and the Emperor Frederick Barbarossa. Himmler would then insist that senior members of the SS join him there for periodic 'spiritual retreats'.

Comical though this is, it is also an accurate manifestation of Himmler's belief that the SS, and particularly the Waffen-SS, was meant to be a monastic warrior order with deliberate echoes of the medieval Crusading Orders such as the Templars, Hospitallers and of course the Germanic Teutonic Knights. Crucially for Himmler's fantasies these medieval orders were international in make-up, organisations defined by their cause rather than by the strict nationality of their adherents. Such examples fuelled Himmler's critical decision to throw the Waffen-SS open to non-Germans. Himmler also saw the world in terms of competing gene pools. His theory was that these gene pools were destined to fight it out through history, with global domination the prize for the winner, and racial extinction for the losers. For the Nazis the Germans were the Aryans, the *Herrenvolk*, the master race of Nazi propaganda. However, while Germany was the undoubted bastion for the Aryan *Herrenvolk*, as a genetic pool they were to be found all over the world. Over hundreds of years racial Germans had established communities across eastern Europe and Russia. These 'Volksdeutsche' were found in large numbers in Hungary, Rumania, Czechoslovakia, Yugoslavia and even as far away as the Volga river region in southern Russia. In terms of non-German Aryans, the Scandinavian and Nordic countries, the Netherlands, Flanders, Luxembourg and Alsace-Lorraine were all home to Aryans, and of course England – NOT Britain as Himmler distinguished between Anglo-Saxon England and the Celtic nature of the Welsh, Irish and Scots. This theory then further extended to England's 'white' colonies of South Africa, Australia and New Zealand, and indeed even to the United States of America. Himmler believed it was his mission to unite all those of Aryan blood across the globe to face the twin threats to their racial survival of communism and international Jewry. These fellow Aryans were to be welcomed into the Waffen-SS family as the 'Freiwilligen'. Himmler explained his views to Arthur Sigailis of the German-sponsored Latvian Legion.

> He [Himmler] then singled out those nations which he regarded as belonging to the German family of nations and they were: the Germans, the Dutch, the Flemish, the Anglo-Saxons, the Scandinavians and the Baltic people. 'To combine all of these nations into one big family is the most important task at the present time' [Himmler said]. This unification has to take place on the principle of equality and at that same time has to secure the identity of each nation and its economical independence, of course, adjusting the latter to the interests of the whole German living space ... After the unification of all the German nations into one family, this family ... has to take over the mission to include, in the family, all the Roman nations whose living space is favoured by nature with a milder climate ... I am convinced that after the unification, the Roman nations will be able to persevere as the Germans.'[1]

These twin pillars of the Volksdeutsche and foreign volunteers, the Freiwilligen, would then become key building blocks in Himmler's growing Waffen-SS.

The Freiwilligen

To an extent the Reichsführer-SS was also acknowledging an existent reality, in that there is evidence that individual foreigners served in the Waffen-SS from the earliest days. However, with the conquest of most of western Europe complete by the end of the summer of 1940, Himmler was able to begin his grand experiment with an appeal to the youth of non-German, but suitably Aryan, nations to join the newly-authorised Waffen-SS national legions. These units were usually based around adherents of local far Right political parties, such as Vidkun Quisling's Nasjonal Samlung (National Union) in Norway, and Sven Olov Lindholm's Svensk Socialistik Samling (Swedish Socialist Union) in Sweden. The best known of these units were the Volunteer Legion Norwegen (Norwegian); Volunteer Legion Flandern (Belgian Flemish); Volunteer Legion Niederlande (Dutch) and the Freikorps Danmark (Danish).

The Legions served on the Eastern Front, following Germany's invasion of the Soviet Union, distinguishing themselves by their bravery and exemplary service, and eventually coalesced in the mainstream divisional structure of the Waffen-SS, in units such as the 5th SS Panzer Division Wiking. This division was based on a German cadre from the SSVT's Germania Regiment with its ranks filled with volunteers from Scandinavia and the Low Countries. Wiking went on to become a first class combat formation rated alongside other premier Waffen-SS units such as the Leibstandarte and Das Reich, with an enviable reputation for bravery and fighting excellence. However, not all the national legions were recruited from such impeccable Aryan stock. Volunteers also came forward from the French-speaking half of Belgium, the Walloons; from France itself, from Dr Anté Pavelic's allied puppet state of Croatia, and even from Franco's Spain. All of these volunteers were steered firmly by Himmler to the Wehrmacht, as he considered them racially unsuitable for the Waffen-SS. The Walloon volunteers joined the Legion Wallonie and were almost all members of the extreme right wing Catholic and nationalist Cristus Rex Party, headed up by its charismatic leader Léon Degrelle. Incidents such as the infamous massacre of twenty-two Belgian right wing political leaders, in a public park in Abbeville, France in May 1940 by French police, helped propel Rex Party members into open collaboration with the Nazis. Degrelle himself joined the Legion Wallonie as a ranker and served with distinction during its battles on the Russian Front, including in the brutal fighting and breakout from the Cherkassy Pocket. He eventually went on to command the Walloons and became the most influential foreign figure in the entire SS legionary movement.

The Croatian volunteers were the Poglavnik's (Anté Pavelic's Croatian title and his version of Führer) contribution to Hitler's war in the East, and were grouped in the Croatian Legion, while the ever wily Generalissimo

Francisco Franco agreed only to a limited number of Spanish troops forming the Blue (Azul) Division for combat in Russia. Franco was prepared to show willing, but nothing else, and even these men were withdrawn by Franco when the tide of war turned. Despite this some Spaniards decided to fight on and several hundred ended up as Waffen-SS members, with a few fighting in Berlin as the war came to a bloody close. Those captured by the Red Army at the very end weren't released for return to Spain until 1954.

Waffen-SS expansion

While this infusion of new blood from Aryan countries helped the Waffen-SS to expand exponentially, it could still not cope with the monumental level of slaughter on the Russian Front. For example, from the launch of Operation Barbarossa on 22 June 1941 up to the end of November 1944, the Germans lost 1,419,728 men killed, 997,056 men missing and 3,498,060 men wounded on the Eastern Front. To put that in context, that is more men than Great Britain and the United States lost in total throughout the war on all Fronts. Nazi Germany needed men, and was becoming far less fussy about where they came from. The fight in the East was also proving an attractive cause to non-Aryan anti-communists, and it was in that context that it became more and more acceptable for Frenchmen to fight alongside the Germans for the first time in the war.

Note

1. Memoirs of Arthur Sigailis, chief of staff of the Inspection General of the Latvian Legion in his book *The Latvian Legion* (James Bender Publishing, 1986).

CHAPTER V

Frenchmen on the Eastern Front: The LVF

The story of Frenchmen serving in the German military was, as in all things the Nazis did, complex, convoluted and ever changing. Himmler's bizarre racial fantasies may have excluded a mainstream French unit from the Waffen-SS in 1941, but it did not exclude it from the order of battle of the Heer. Even then these rules were not hard and fast, as Alsatians, Lorrainians and other individuals of French blood entered the Waffen-SS in the opening years of the war on a host of often flimsy pretexts. The situation was akin to that of France's own famous Foreign Legion in which Frenchmen are barred from entry (except as officers), but many Frenchmen have always served in the ranks, citing their nationality as Belgian, Swiss, Luxembourgers, and even French speakers from overseas. Numbers joining the Waffen-SS under such circumstances were small admittedly, and because of the subterfuge impossible to detail, but it is estimated that around 300 Frenchmen enlisted under the subterfuge of 'Flemings born in Northern France' (*Ch'timi* for short) in the years 1940 and 1941. These men went on to serve mainly in the elite Totenkopf and Wiking Divisions prior to Himmler's belated agreement to the establishment of a French Waffen-SS unit in late 1943.

However, the Heer, Luftwaffe, Kriegsmarine and a host of other Nazi military and indeed paramilitary organisations tended to be far more practical in their outlook than Reichsführer-SS Himmler. The uniformed labour service, the Organization Todt, was happy to accept French volunteers, as were several other service units such as the Teno and NSKK that recruited Frenchmen as uniformed drivers, mechanics and logistics personnel. Yet more volunteers enlisted as sailors in the Kriegsmarine, and these men were mainly drawn from France's traditional seafaring communities in Normandy, Brittany and the Atlantic Coast. The Luftwaffe benefited from French volunteers acting as ground support staff, though there is no evidence of any Frenchmen flying combat missions. There was even a small, though unknown, number of Frenchmen operating in the shadowy world of German special forces in both the Army's Brandenburger units and in the SS operating under the leadership of that talismanic character, Otto Skorzeny.

The LVF is born

There was a varied and colourful panorama of French military service with the Third Reich in the early years of the war. However, the unit that came to epitomise French military collaboration with the Germans, and became instrumental in the later birth and development of Charlemagne, was the Légion des Volontaires Français contre le bolchevisme, the LVF for short. Doriot in particular, allied with the pro-French German Ambassador in Paris, Otto Abetz, had been agitating for some time for the creation of a French unit that would fight alongside the Germans. This unit would be overtly political in its membership and would be the French version of the SS, in terms of being the uniformed standard bearers of the 'new France'. While being an official French military formation, it would be used to combat the threat of communism, both at home and abroad and would give military legitimacy to the political aspirations of France's far Right.

At first the Nazis viewed the idea with little more than a polite lack of interest. Nazi policy was heavily influenced by Francophobes such as Goering and there was no appetite for the promotion of a resurgent French national fighting force, quite the opposite in fact. However, following the appalling slaughter of the Eastern Front, the Nazi position modified drastically and consent was given for the raising of an anti-communist French military unit. But the Germans insisted on certain caveats: firstly numbers were to be restricted to a maximum of 15,000 in total, with a frontline strength not to exceed 3,000 soldiers; and secondly, as clearly stated under international law, the unit was to wear *German* uniform when outside France as France had not actually declared war on Soviet Russia; and lastly the unit was to come strictly under German control at all times. The only distinguishing feature permitted was that a French tricolour arm shield with the word 'France' at the top, or LVF at the bottom, was to be worn on the right sleeve of the standard German Army uniform. These restrictions dismayed and angered many proponents and would-be volunteers for the unit, but they were accepted as necessary evils under which the French would have to serve. So on 7 July 1941 a meeting was held between the leaders of the main collaborationist parties, including Doriot and Déat, at the Hôtel Majestic in Paris. Agreement was reached on the formation of the unit and a *comité central de LVF* under Deloncle of the extremist Mouvement Social Révolutionnaire (MSR) was established. The following day a recruiting office was set up in the former Soviet tourist office building at 12 rue Auber, in Paris's 9th district. The French party political leaders then proceeded to sell the idea to their party members and encourage sign-up. On 18 July a mass rally was held at the Vélodrome d'Hiver with speeches by both Doriot and Deloncle. Estimates put attendance at over 10,000, though many were women and so unable to volunteer for service. Deloncle declared boldly: 'Europe is on the march, nothing will stop it!'

As for Doriot himself, he demonstrated that he was that rarest of political animals, a politician who practised what he preached. He stood up, announced the foundation of the LVF, and committed himself to joining up and called on his supporters to follow his example. But it was notable that there was less enthusiasm than the party leaders had anticipated among their rank and file. Notwithstanding that, recruitment was acceptable enough and by the end of August 1941 some 13,400 volunteers had come forward. As ever with the German military, particularly on the dentistry side(!), there was a considerable weeding out process, and in the end only 5,800 volunteers were accepted for training. That was an acceptance rate of less than 45% when there was a war on and Germany was losing tens of thousands of men every month (51,000 killed in the month of July 1941 alone).

As for Doriot, he went to Russia with the LVF, was wounded, and subsequently invalided back to France in 1943. Here he continued his political collaboration, acting as a thorn in Vichy's side as he exhorted his fellow Frenchmen and women to actively support the Germans in the fight against Bolshevism.

Deba and the LVF at the gates of Moscow

A former regular French Army officer with little field experience, Colonel Roger Labonne, was appointed the first Commanding Officer of the LVF on 20 August 1941, and he presided over the ceremony at Versailles on the 27th of the same month when the LVF formally received its first colour standard. This parade was mostly remembered for the startling act of one of the volunteers who fired on the party of dignitaries assembled for the occasion, in the process wounding both Déat and Pierre Laval. The following month, on 4 September, the first batch of twenty-five officers and 803 NCOs and other ranks embarked for their training base at Deba in conquered Poland. They would become the Legion's 1st Battalion. A second contingent of a further 127 officers and 769 NCOs and other ranks left France on 29 September bound to join up with their erstwhile comrades at Deba. They would become the 2nd Battalion. A third draft of twenty-one officers and 623 NCOS and other ranks would arrive in Deba on 12 October 1941.

At the Deba Training Camp the LVF became a distinctly French outfit, albeit in German uniform. There was no adoption of Germanic standards

Battles of the LVF and the SS-Sturmbrigade 1941–1944

of discipline and conduct, but rather a self-conscious parading of the 'Frenchness' of the LVF with a certain casual attitude to uniform dress codes, the formalities of rank and the book of military regulations. There is no lack of fighting military tradition in France though, and the legionnaires trained hard to become operationally ready for combat on the Russian Front. Many had previous military service in the French armed forces, so that by the end of October 1941, after less than two months' training, the LVF was passed fit for active service.

Officially designated the Infanterieregiment 638 des Heeres, the 638th Reinforced French Infantry Regiment, it left Deba at the end of October *en route* for the Russian Front. Arriving in Smolensk, the LVF foot marched eastwards to the Front where it was assigned to the German 7th Infantry Division, part of Army Group B, fighting near Golovko in front of Moscow. There it was part of Operation Typhoon, the belated German drive to capture Moscow. The LVF was organised into two combat battalions, comprising 181 officers and 2,271 NCOs and other ranks, with a total of thirty-five German liaison staff. The two battalions had four infantry companies each, with attached light artillery and anti-tank companies as well as various support sub-units.

On 1 December in the deep snow and bitter cold of the horrendous Russian winter of 1941–2, the LVF went into combat for the very first time when the 1st Battalion mounted an attack on the Russian lines. The attack was a partial success and nothing more. Some ground was taken from the Soviets, and a number of Russians were killed and captured. The LVF suffered its first ever casualties in the attack of twelve men killed and fifty-five wounded; they would not be its last.

The LVF mirrored its German Army brethren by being hopelessly ill-equipped for the sub-zero temperatures and near Arctic conditions of winter on the Russian steppes. That winter of 1941-2 was also the worst on record for nearly half a century, and the invaders suffered mightily. All along the thousands of kilometres of the German Front casualties from frostbite mounted alarmingly, sentries froze to death at their posts, gun mechanisms jammed and engines and machinery froze up. The much-vaunted German war machine ground to a halt, and so did the Frenchmen of the LVF. Still clad in inadequate summer clothing, the Germans and Frenchmen huddled together for warmth in their miserable dugouts waiting for the weather to change. For the Russians this was their opportunity, and they took it.

From intelligence reports the STAVKA, Soviet High Command, had found out that the Japanese had no intention of striking their Soviet neighbours, preferring instead to attack the United Sates. This realisation allowed the Russians to redeploy their well-equipped Siberian rifle divisions from the Far East Command for service against the Germans in front of Moscow. These units were well used to operating in the terrible winter conditions, and were equipped and trained to do so.

Massing the newly-arrived Siberians and their new T-34 super tanks together, the Russians launched their huge winter counter-offensive against the overstretched and exhausted German lines. Typhoon was smashed and the Germans were sent reeling backwards. Unit after unit was wiped out or decimated in the snows and all along the Front the fighting was desperate. The LVF was heavily involved, fighting off attack after attack from the suddenly numerous and well-equipped Red Army. Like its German counterparts the LVF was told by Hitler to hold, not to yield one yard of ground, but to fight to the last man and the last bullet. This was a seemingly mad order at the time, but it was one designed to avoid the fate of Napoleon's Grande Armeé of 1812 in being slaughtered in the snow in a horrific retreat.

The German line held, but the price was high. By the end of January 1942 the LVF had lost half of its original strength after little more than two months of combat. There was to be no respite. In February 1942 disaster struck when the much-reduced 2nd Battalion was caught in a Soviet assault near the town of Djunovo. The battalion was isolated, overrun and virtually wiped out. The few remaining survivors who managed to escape the slaughter were withdrawn to Kruszyna in Poland, along with the 1st Battalion, for reorganisation. Here the two battalions were merged into one nominally full strength unit. At that stage the LVF had not covered itself in glory according to its German masters, indeed Goebbels wrote of it: '...the Frenchmen had in no way distinguished themselves on the Eastern Front.'

Anti-partisan warfare

Following the massacre at Djunovo and the subsequent reorganisation, the inadequate Labonne was relieved of command and recalled to Paris in March. The newly-merged battalion was taken off front-line combat duties, and instead was redeployed in an anti-partisan role behind the Front. Its new commander was a Major Lacroix. Meanwhile, back in Deba a further four drafts of volunteers had arrived between December 1941 and February 1942 and had undergone training. They were then formed into a 3rd Battalion under the command of a Colonel Ducrot, quickly replaced on the grounds of incompetence by Major Demessine, and then sent to Russia. From then on the two LVF battalions operated independently of each other in the rear of Army Group Centre where they fought against the partisans. By June 1942 the 1st Battalion was attached to the German 186th Security Division and was fighting partisans near Smolensk, while the 3rd was in action around Volost with the 221st Security Division, where it sustained heavy casualties in operations against large concentrations of guerrillas. As elsewhere in occupied Russia very often significant numbers of Red Army personnel had been left behind German lines in the mass defeats and retreats of 1941, and they had turned themselves into partisan formations of considerable size. It was not uncommon for partisan units to be of brigade size or above in the vast and trackless forests and marshes.

It was also in the summer of 1942, on 18 July, that Marshal Pétain's Vichy Government officially recognised the battlefield decoration of the LVF, the Croix de Guerre Légionnaire. This act was hugely symbolic in granting the LVF legitimacy and official recognition, and was a further muddying of the waters in talk of treason and patriotism in wartime France.

The two French LVF battalions continued to carry out their separate, but similar, combat roles until June 1943 when the 3rd Battalion was finally regrouped together with the 1st under the command of General Oschmann's 286th Security Division in the Moghilev and Orsha region of central Russia. The 2nd Battalion was reformed with new replacements, and the whole unit reorganised into the French Grenadier Regiment 638.

A new commander

Most significantly the LVF received a new French Commanding Officer, Colonel Edgar Puaud. He was unlike the unfortunate Labonne in having a significant record of combat service. Edgar-Joseph-Alexandre Puaud was born on 29 October 1889 in the city of Orléans. He was a career soldier, having enlisted in 1909 in the infantry, and went on to serve with distinction in World War I winning a drawer full of medals, including the Croix de Guerre and the Légion d'honneur and winning promotion to officer rank. In the inter-war years he served abroad with the Foreign Legion in the French Empire in Morocco and Tonkin, until finally returning to metropolitan France in 1939. He didn't receive a fighting command as France prepared to fight Germany for a second time that century, but instead watched his beloved Army crushed and his nation conquered. A French patriot and convinced supporter of Vichy, he went on to serve in the Armistice Army before joining Le Légion Tricolore. It was from here that he came to the LVF.

Following Puaud's assumption of command, in October of the same year the light artillery sub-unit was disbanded and a new 4th Battalion of infantry formed instead. There were now some sixteen companies of French infantry serving on the Russian Front. Further anti-partisan actions were fought including the large-scale Operation Morocco in January 1944 near Somry. That operation, named in honour of Colonel Puaud's previous service history, resulted in 1,118 Soviet partisans killed and a further

1,345 captured. Of important note here is the absence of any reported atrocity by the French units involved.

The partisan war fought in Russia was one marked by brutal savagery on an almost medieval scale by both sides. It was common for Soviet partisans to horrifically mutilate and butcher any prisoners who fell into their hands, and the Nazis characterised their operations by the mass murder of civilians. Yet the French were involved in combating the partisans for a considerable time and did not succumb to the tactics of butchery and atrocity as practised by so many in Soviet Russia on both sides. This lack of attributed atrocities is a theme that recurred in the combat record of the subsequent formations of the SS-Sturmbrigade Frankreich and in Charlemagne, and led to a blemish-free reputation for the French volunteers who served alongside the Germans. This was incredibly rare, when even elites such as the Leibstandarte and Das Reich had their Malmédy and Oradour.

Bobr – cometh the hour

The days of the LVF fighting partisans came to an end in June 1944 when the entire regiment was assembled to be sent back to France; coincidentally this was exactly the same time that the newly-raised SS-Sturmbrigade Frankreich was being readied for action in the East. However, it was now that fate stepped in and enabled the LVF to truly distinguish itself in a way that it had been unable to for the previous two and a half years. The Soviets launched their massive summer offensive of 1944, Operation Bagration, and the German Front was completely sundered. In desperation the German High Command threw every available unit and soldier into the line to try to hold the front. This included the LVF who were thrust back into the line to combat the Russian juggernaut that was tearing the Germans into bloody shreds.

A composite unit comprising the 1st Battalion and two companies of the 3rd Battalion, under the command of Major Eugene-Marie-Jean Bridoux (the professional soldier son of the Vichy Minister for War, General Bridoux), took up a defensive position overlooking a key bridge over the Bobr river on the vitally important main Minsk–Moscow highway. If the bridge was captured by the Russians and the highway cut, then the entire German 9th Army would be encircled and annihilated. The Frenchmen were joined in their defence by some 600 German soldiers, and over a desperate forty-eight hours the mixed German-French kampfgruppe held attack after attack by overwhelming numbers of Russians. Supported by a small number of tanks, with limited air support, the French legionnaires stood their ground and fought hand-to-hand with waves of Soviet tanks and infantry. The Russians also knew how important the bridge was and were determined to take it. Massed Soviet artillery pounded the

French positions to be followed every time by waves of Soviets screaming their wild '*Urrahs!*' Trenches were lost to the charging Russians and then retaken at the point of the bayonet by ever fewer legionnaires, but the position held. So ferocious was the French defence that the Soviet High Command, the STAVKA, reported that it believed a force of 'two French divisions' were involved in opposing it.

On the morning of 27 June the remaining Frenchmen were finally relieved and they pulled back to new positions near Borisov. Their defiance had a price though, and they left over forty of their number dead on the Bobr. But the Russians had paid a far higher price and more than forty Soviet tanks were burning in front of the French trenches.

Over the next couple of weeks the exhausted legionnaires were hit again and again by renewed Soviet attacks and, lacking heavy weapons, were smashed by massed Soviet tank assaults. Casualties were huge, but in July orders were finally received to pull back to Greifenberg in Pomerania for a desperately needed rest and refit.

At last the LVF had distinguished itself. The battle over the Bobr was hugely significant for the LVF. The previous years of duty in the East had seen the LVF act competently, but had not seen it achieve any sort of renown. Removed from front-line combat, the arena of anti-partisan warfare was not one in which legends were established, except infamous ones such as the SS Dirlewanger Brigade due to their atrocious record of massacre and brutality, and there was little opportunity for the Frenchmen to build any sort of fighting tradition or *esprit de corps*. What Bobr did was enable the LVF to have its own legend, its own Alamo, that its members could take with it into the Charlemagne.

The end of the LVF

For the LVF it was the end of the road. Himmler now looked with enthusiasm on the idea of French Waffen-SS men and, as ever, his mind was turning to the expansion of his own power base. As the LVF had been fighting the partisans and then on the Bobr, there had been huge changes in the position of Frenchmen fighting with the Germans, and there was now an SS-Sturmbrigade Frankreich composed of French Waffen-SS men. Himmler now reasoned it made sense to group all Frenchmen serving in the German armed forces together in a new Waffen-SS division if possible. The idea of Charlemagne was born, and with it died the old LVF. There was no room for both a Heer-sponsored unit like the LVF, and a French Waffen-SS division, particularly in view of Himmler's drive to ever expand his SS empire. So on 1 September 1944, after more than three years of life, Le Légion des Volontaires Français contre le bolchevisme was officially disbanded, and its members were 'offered' service in the new SS Division instead. In reality only officers had any choice in their transferral, and those who objected were released from the service. For the privates and NCOs there was no such luxury and they were effectively press-ganged into the Waffen-SS. There was, unsurprisingly, a certain amount of disgruntlement among the legionnaires about their situation, but most swallowed their anger and drew on their new uniforms with their Waffen-SS tricolour badges on the upper left sleeve and not the right as in the LVF. Some, however did not, and even after being cajoled, shouted at and threatened, refused to serve. They ended up in a Nazi labour camp.

In total some 6,429 volunteers were accepted into the LVF during its existence. In the first half of its life up to the end of May 1943, first in front of Moscow and then against the partisans, the LVF lost a total of 169 men killed and 550 wounded. In its second eighteen months of service, beginning with more anti-partisan fighting and ending on the Bobr and in Operation Bagration, casualties were far, far higher with over 400 further legionnaires killed in action. This was a direct reflection of the fierceness of the fighting in which the LVF was involved, in particular at the Bobr and trying to stave off the Soviets in the days after that epic struggle. In a couple of weeks the LVF sustained as many casualties as it had in almost nine months of fighting against Soviet partisans. Over the course of its short life the LVF had served continuously on the Russian Front for three years, almost since the beginning of Operation Barbarossa, and more than one in ten of its legionnaires were buried there on the vast steppes and in the endless, trackless forests of Russia.

Of our three leading characters only Pierre Rostaing served in the LVF. He joined with the sixth tranche of volunteers, having been demobilised for a third time following the disbandment of Le Légion Tricolore. He then spent three months with his fellow recruits carrying out training at Deba in Poland, prior to deployment to the Russian Front. Having been put through the rigours of German Army training, Rostaing was then posted to the 9th Company of the 3rd Battalion serving in its anti-partisan role to the rear of Army Group Centre. As one of the company's senior NCOs he fought against Russian partisan bands and distinguished himself, to the point where he was posted internally to the battalion's *section de chasse*, basically the unit's premier partisan 'hunting' platoon. It was this platoon that spearheaded all the battalion's drives against the enemy, firstly sniffing the partisan bands out in their hideouts, and initially engaging them. Once pinned by the fire of the platoon the rest of the battalion were thrown around their prey as a noose or brought into the fight headlong to smash the enemy. These were the tactics of search, pin and destroy that the LVF tried hard to perfect during its long and deadly games of cat and mouse with the bands of guerrillas.

In this sub-unit he served under the platoon command of a Lieutenant Seveau who appreciated Rostaing's professionalism and coolness under fire. He was duly rewarded by being appointed to be the platoon's senior NCO, its sergent-chef. In this role Rostaing continued to demonstrate his military prowess, until he and his platoon were selected as part of Major Bridoux's Kampfgruppe for the Bobr, where he and his men fought against the endless waves of screaming Russians. Following the LVF's withdrawal from Russia back to Pomerania, Rostaing was recognised as one of the most decorated Frenchmen serving in the German Army. He had already been awarded the Iron Cross 2nd Class on 20 April 1944, in recognition of his bravery, and this award sat alongside the Croix de Guerre Légionnaire, the wounded badge and no fewer than twelve separate citations he had won in combat. Now the LVF was coming to its end, Rostaing's future was in the Waffen-SS and Charlemagne.

CHAPTER VI

Formation of the SS-Sturmbrigade Frankreich

By 1943 not only the Waffen-SS but all of Nazi Germany was desperate for manpower. The response of the Waffen-SS was to change its recruiting pattern and standards once again in order to try to fill the yawning gaps in its still-proud ranks. Nationalities and ethnic groups that would have by no means been considered as fitting the previous SS racial standard were actually appealed to and encouraged to join. Volunteers and their units, that had previously only been considered racially suitable for the Heer, were transferred en masse to the Waffen-SS on Himmler's direct intervention. The stringent terms of service for Waffen-SS recruits were dramatically relaxed to encourage volunteers, with enlistment being shortened to two years, or the duration of war (usually whichever was the longest). But these volunteers were not considered full members of the Waffen-SS, nor did they usually take the standard SS oath, though they still pledged direct allegiance to Hitler. They wore variations of standard SS insignia on their uniforms, which indicated their status as non-Germans, and highlighted their differentiation from full Waffen-SS members. They only had to meet the barest of military entry standards and there was no ideological acceptance threshold either. This was a far cry from the original image of the Waffen-SS as the physical, racial and ideological standard bearers of Nazism.

This was the background to Hitler's decision of 30 January 1943 when he finally authorised the recruitment of Frenchmen directly into the Waffen-SS. A recruiting office was hastily set up at 24 avenue du Recteur-Poincaré in the 16th district of Paris, and senior German and French figures debated the establishment, size and nomenclature of the new unit. Initially at least it was decided to raise a regimental-sized grouping (a German regiment was equivalent in size to a British brigade and/or a Russian division), and name it Karl der Grosse, the German name for the Holy Roman Frankish Emperor, Charlemagne. On the French side, Pierre Laval,

the chief minister of the Vichy Government, promulgated a law sanction-
ing the direct enlistment of French citizens into the Waffen-SS. This new
law sanctioned the actions of volunteers citing the same reasoning as was
used in the raising of the old LVF. The French Waffen-SS were afforded
the same official recognition as the LVF legionnaires, and were given the
same benefits and privileges. So joining the Waffen-SS was now officially
legal in France!

Entry requirements were not as strict as for pre-war German Waffen-SS
recruits, but were modelled on the criteria employed by the LVF. Volunteers
had to be physically fit, be a minimum of 165cm tall (3cm shorter than
German standards), and be aged between 17 and 40. You were disbarred
from joining by having Jewish blood, or having been deprived of your
civil rights by the French government for a serious criminal offence.

To head the new formation the Germans turned to a 58-year-old Breton
and former lieutenant-colonel in the French Army, Paul-Marie Gamory-
Dubordeau. Whilst it was recognised by the Germans that the majority of
volunteers would probably come from the collaborationist French political
parties, they also understood that the officer corps the unit needed would
almost certainly not come from the same source. The rightist parties were
strongly working-class, and very few would either have served as officers
in the French armed forces, or be of the requisite calibre to become officers
in the new unit. The SS-Sturmbrigade Frankreich really needed qualified
and experienced ex-officers from the French Army to act as its cadre if it
was to become operational anytime soon, and the simple fact was that
such men were to be found in large numbers in the Milice, and not in
the likes of the MSR, PPF or PSF. However the Germans were also keen
to avoid the avowedly nationalist and anti-German Milice dominating
the new force, and so cast their net wider for a commander who would
counter-balance the influence of Darnard's men.

They found such a man in Gamory-Dubordeau. Approaching 60 years
old he might have been, but he was experienced, energetic and an ardent
member of Doriot's PPF. Born on 29 January 1885 in the small town of
Ploudalmezeau in the far west of Brittany, Gamory-Dubordeau began
his military career in that crucible of professional soldiering, the Foreign
Legion. He attended the infantry school at Saint-Maxient and graduated as
a second lieutenant in 1911, where his first posting was to the 2nd Colonial
Infantry Regiment based in Brest. He then went on to serve in the Camel
Corps and the Supply Corps, in postings all over the Empire including
stints in the Sudan and Morocco. After leaving the service as a lieutenant-colonel he joined the PPF, and rose to become its Assistant-Secretary
in Morocco. He was also something of a Breton nationalist, and he led a
small activist group called 'Le Roc breton' that agitated for greater Breton
autonomy. The Germans did not envisage Gamory-Dubordeau leading

the new unit in combat, but rather saw him as a coordinating figurehead who was far more controllable than either Darnard or Doriot.

Recruitment drive

Recruitment was encouraged by the Germans from the same organisations whose members filled the ranks of the then-existant LVF. These were mainly the collaborationist parties of the French far Right including the PPF, the RNP, the PSF and the MSR, and in particular the various youth wings of these parties. Efforts were also made to recruit among the large numbers of French STO workers in Germany, from other Frenchmen serving the Germans in various branches of the armed forces, and of course the Milice. All of these reservoirs of potential recruits were tapped with varying degrees of success, with Doriot's PPF again proving themselves most amenable to the recruiting drive. Despite considerable pressure from the Germans the Milice proved surprisingly resistant to the recruiters and provided only a few hundred men.

An analysis carried out by the Germans on a batch of French recruits in December of 1943 found that 20% were from the PPF, 4% from the rival RNP, 28% from other collaborationist parties, with 38% having no party affiliation at all. Only 10% of the sample was from the Milice. Geographically, recruits from Paris dominated, making up 28% of the volunteers. As the number of ex-Miliciens increased there would be a watering down of this Parisian dominance, as the Milice was strongest in the south of France, but it was never wholly eradicated.

The recruits came from an astonishing number of countries, as ex-colonists volunteered from all corners of the vast French Empire. Men enlisted who were born in central, north and west Africa, French Indochina (present day Vietnam, Laos and Cambodia) and even Sri Lanka. The LVF had accepted North African black recruits, just as the French Army did with its profusion of units recruited from native populations, but this was not going to be the case in the Waffen-SS. Even so a black legionnaire from Martinique, Norbert Désiré, tried to transfer to the SS but unsurprisingly he was not accepted, and was actually sent to a labour camp along with those legionnaires who refused to transfer. The authorities didn't know what to do with him!

Initial recruitment was not at the same high levels among some other nationalities, such as the Ukrainians, Dutch and Balts, but was still encouraging enough for the Germans, particularly given their dire need for manpower. Indeed over 1,500 volunteers came forward by 30 September 1943. However even at this late stage of the war, and with so many restrictions being relaxed, selection was still unbelievably rigorous with only roughly a third of these volunteers being accepted into the Waffen-SS and sent to the camp at Sennheim, in Alsace-Lorraine, for basic training. Undoubtedly the dentistry obsession came into full force yet again!

From the start though it was made clear to all the volunteers that this wasn't a 'new' LVF, but something entirely different. This unit was to be Waffen-SS in body and soul. The French nationalist overtones of the LVF were to give way for the birth of a unit that was to be truly 'European' in feel. One of the volunteers was the 19-year-old Jean de Misser, a young man with no party political connections, who was placed in the 1st Platoon of SS-Obersturmführer's (lieutenant), Sommer's 5th Company. De Misser said the following on the training and feel of the new unit; his comments are very instructive:

> My instructors were in the image of the Waffen-SS: European. My sec-
> tion commander was a Flemish Rottenführer [corporal] and my platoon
> commander an Oberscharführer [colour sergeant] from Luxembourg.

It was obvious then that this unit was going to be a break with the past. The Regiment would not be made to be German, but would be firmly modelled on the best of the so-called 'Aryan' Waffen-SS units, such as the Wiking and Nordland Divisions. The lessons learned on a hundred battlefields on the Russian steppes would be used to turn these raw French recruits into a unit fit to stand in the line with the legends of the Waffen-SS. But from the start it was obvious that the greatest enemy the new regiment had to face, even before it reached the Front, was time.

Any soldier will tell you that every day spent on the training grounds prior to active service is invaluable, and this is particularly true for any unit being raised from scratch. If a recruit is being trained to join an established unit then this is by far an easier process. The instructors know that they can concentrate on instilling the basics, confident that the soldier will complete his 'schooling' with his mates, his corporals, and most of all from his platoon sergeant and platoon commander when he reaches his unit. This unit as a 'finishing school' is one of the reasons that the premier Waffen-SS divisions, such as the Leibstandarte and Das Reich, could continue to operate to such high standards despite suffering catastrophic losses during the war.

The losses to the Waffen-SS were so great that it was not uncommon for the divisions to be decimated and rebuilt a few times over during the course of the war. For example the 3rd SS Panzer Division Totenkopf had an established strength of approximately 19,700 personnel when fully manned. During the war it suffered over 60,000 casualties, but was still able to remain a premier fighting formation. Even the 5th SS Panzer Division Wiking, which came into being much later than the Totenkopf, lost more than 19,000 men during its short life.

The process then, was clear and successful. Young Waffen-SS recruits would leave their training depots and join their units, and there would learn from those around them how to survive and how to fight. The French Freiwilligen, critically, did not have this luxury. Their initial incarnation as the Französisches SS-Freiwilligen-Grenadier-Regiment, from October to November 1943, was as a unit created from nothing, with a minimum cadre of experienced Waffen-SS personnel. French-speaking Alsatians serving in other Waffen-SS units were drafted in to stiffen the ranks, an unpopular move with the draftees, but one that would pay off in combat and at least give the French volunteers a chance later on. However, it is a fact that this lack of time was to dog the French SS right through from its days as a new unit to its final bow as Charlemagne, and cause many a volunteer's death at the Front.

Karl der Grosse to Sturmbrigade Frankreich

Back in the complex world of political rivalry in Vichy France, a world away from the frenzied preparation and training in Sennheim, the old battles were being fought anew. Pétain was still determined to remain aloof in splendid isolation from the parties of the far Right and was still blocking the inclusion of Doriot and his PPF in government. Doriot's only comfort was that his bitter rival Marcel Déat, and his RNP, were also out in the political cold. But these parties, and particularly their youth wings, were still important sources of possible recruits for any Waffen-SS unit such as the Französisches SS Regiment. As for Darnard and his Milice they were coming under increasing pressure from a resistance movement that was finally starting to make an impression. Their initial status as unarmed guardians of order marked them out as soft targets, and they were suffering increasingly from close-quarter assassination. Miliciens learned to fear the knock on their front door late at night; was it an innocent visitor or was it a team of *maquisards*? If it was the latter a bullet in the head was what awaited the awakened Milicien as he opened the door. In or out of uniform the Miliciens were marked out in their communities, and always had one eye watching over their shoulder.

As volunteers were sent to Sennheim, Nazi bureaucracy continued to churn and the still-forming unit was re-designated several times, being called a bewildering variety of names and unit titles, including a period as the Karl der Grosse Regiment, but eventually it settled down as the Französisches SS-Freiwilligen-Regiment 57 in November 1943. They would retain this title until July 1944, when they were finally incarnated as an SS volunteer assault brigade, called either the Französisches SS-Freiwilligen-Sturmbrigade or the Französisches SS-Sturmbrigade Nr. 8, hereafter referred to simply as SS-Sturmbrigade Frankreich.

The nomenclature of a unit's designation was crucially important in the Waffen-SS as there were clear distinctions between the different racial categories of members. These may seem purely bureaucratic and faintly ridiculous, but in the fantasy world of Himmler's racial philosophy there was nothing of greater import. Divisions staffed by Reich Germans had the nomenclature 'SS-Division' while those comprising mainly Volksdeutsche or suitably Aryan Europeans, such as the Scandinavians, were called 'SS-Freiwilligen Division'. Units composed primarily of non-Aryans, East Europeans or Russians came into the category of 'Waffen Division der SS', a term of inferiority which denoted attachment to, rather than actual membership of, the Waffen-SS. This then was the status of the newly-recruited French SS men.

Names to remember
It was here in the SS-Sturmbrigade that two of our three volunteers will meet. Darnard was extremely keen that his Milice was strongly represented, and hopefully dominant, in the new force. Unlike the LVF, which was dominated by party adherents of Doriot and Déat, the new Waffen-SS unit was seen by Darnard as a forerunner for a resurrected French Army earning its place as a partner alongside Germany by fighting the Red menace in the East. Through 1943 and early 1944 Darnard exhorted his men to join, particularly the graduates of the Milice's officer training school at Uriage. Recruitment was not strong however, and throughout 1943 only some 300 Miliciens answered Darnard's call and enlisted. One of those that did was Henri Joseph Fenet. Aged 24, and a trained Milicien officer, Fenet answered the call of his chief and enlisted on 18 October 1943.

For André Bayle his time had come at long last. Even though the official minimum enlistment age was 17 that didn't stop Bayle who presented himself at a recruiting office and wouldn't take no for an answer; he was 16 years old and he was officially the youngest French recruit in the Waffen-SS.

D-Day: the world turns
The political field in France then underwent a seismic shift with the Allied invasion of Normandy on 6 June 1944 – D-Day.

After D-Day and the successful Allied breakout from Normandy, it became clear to those French who had sided with the Germans that they had to abandon France in order to escape both the Allied advance and their fellow-countrymen's retribution. The violent political divisions in France were thrown sharply into focus as the choices available to all Frenchmen became stark. To be with the Resistance, either communist or Free French, was to be with the Western Allies and Soviet Russia. To be with Vichy was to be with the Germans.

With the loss of the Battle for Normandy at Falaise, the Wehrmacht lost France. The defeated Germans streamed north and east abandoning great swathes of the country to the advancing Allies or the local population. An orgy of vengeance, bloodletting and hypocrisy followed as large numbers of Frenchmen and women, who had played no active part in the resistance to the invaders for the previous four years, rushed to prove their patriotism. Young women who had had sexual relationships with Germans were abused and had their hair shaved in public as a sign of their shame; some were even murdered. Anyone else who was viewed as a collaborator or a Pétainist was in the firing line, and top of the list were the Miliciens. Local *résistants*, often only members of the Resistance since D-Day or later, seized every Milicien they could lay their hands on and shot them in the streets. Those Miliciens who escaped the bloodletting formed into convoys, for protection, with their families and headed to the comparative safety of Germany. Many did not make it, being ambushed on the way and killed.

In the chaotic and desperate evacuation, Jacques Doriot managed to flee with a handful of adherents to Sigmaringen, a town in the heart of Würrtemburg that had been designated by the Nazis as the collection point for those Frenchmen still loyal to them, and it was here that Darnard and his remaining followers also washed up. In managing to reach Sigmaringen, Doriot and Darnard were luckier than many other collaborators and their families. The Milice in particular lost many members who weren't quick enough to get out of France following the post-Falaise collapse of the German Army.

On arrival Darnard tried to exert his authority with the Germans, but it was clear his influence was in terminal and rapid decline. Try as he might to play a leading role in the Nazis' future plans for his Milice it was too late. He was consulted out of courtesy, but his views were not heeded. His beloved Milice would be taken into the European Waffen-SS whether he agreed or not. As a sop he was appointed Waffen-Sturmbannführer, but the Nazis were careful to give him no direct leadership role in the emerging Charlemagne Division.

Germany's military situation worsens

Across the continent the German military machine was still functioning but was doing so under increased pressure, particularly in the East. 1941 and the beginning of Operation Barbarossa had seen a victorious Wehrmacht cut swathes through a Red Army still reeling after the barbarity and slaughter of Stalin's purges. The execution or imprisonment of whole generations of officers had comprehensively wrecked the Soviet military, and led to almost innumerable hordes of bewildered Red Army men surrendering to the Wehrmacht in the summers of 1941 and 1942. Those days were now firmly over. In their place was a Red Army filled with confidence, equipped on a lavish scale and with immense reserves of manpower.

Soviet equipment may have lacked the finesse of German engineering but what it lacked in technical excellence it more than made up for in sheer mass. As Stalin himself was fond of pointing out, quantity had a quality all of its own. Soviet doctrine and leadership at all levels had also taken huge strides forward so that German tactical superiority could now no longer be counted on, and as Hitler's micro- and mismanagement of Germany's armed forces grew more acute, so Stalin gave more operational freedom to his increasingly successful officer corps.

Defeat at Kursk in Operation Zitadelle in the summer of 1943 had robbed Germany of the initiative in the East, and by 1944 the Ostheer (German Army in the East) was firmly on the defensive. Now the Germans were being forced to react to a growing wave of hammer blows landed on it by the Red Army. In such circumstances it was only a matter of time before Germany's desperate need for manpower outweighed considerations of adequate training and preparation, and forced the deployment to the East of any units that could be found. The days of the SS-Sturmbrigade at Sennheim were numbered.

The summer of 1944: the LVF and the SS-Sturmbrigade

It was Operation Bagration, the great Soviet summer offensive of 1944, that linked the legionnaires of the LVF and their Waffen-SS compatriots in the SS-Sturmbrigade Frankreich. For the LVF it saw them finally establish a fighting reputation on the banks of the Bobr river astride the Smolensk–Minsk highway, when Bridoux and his men stood and held the Russians in Belorussia. Bagration was also a turning point for the SS-Sturmbrigade. Here, hundreds of miles south and west of the legionnaires of the LVF, they would fight, and start building their own legend. So it was that, although separated by the huge distances typical of the Eastern Front, these two units would fight their major battles in the same summer in response to the same Soviet offensive threat. When these two units then came together there would at least be a common thread. But first the French SS men had to earn their spurs down at the junction of Poland and the Ukraine, in Galicia.

CHAPTER VII

French SS First Blood: Galicia

Galicia is the name given to the region that forms the border provinces of north-western Ukraine and southern Poland, At one time most of it was ruled by the sprawling Austro-Hungarian Empire of the Habsburg monarchy until after World War I. There is no Galician ethnic group as such, with the area inhabited by both Poles and Ukrainians, and these two communities are fiercely proud of their own different national heritages, with the Ukrainians especially being of a strongly nationalist bent.

War was nothing new in Galicia; the region had been fought over for centuries and was now in the eye of the storm again. The terrain is one of rolling plains and thick forests, with the only major obstacles to massed military movement being the Vistula and San rivers that run roughly south–north through the area. While not being an area of wide open steppe, as found farther east in Russia, it was still eminently suitable for modern manoeuvre warfare. Towns and villages were then relatively few and far apart, and the only conurbations of any appreciable size were Lwow, Lublin, Chelm and Przemysl. Other places that were to feature in the ensuing battles, such as Sanok, Mielec, Mokré and Radomysl, were little more than small market towns.

Situation report: June–July 1944

Post-D-Day the combined armies of the Western Allies were now on mainland Europe and proceeding to bleed the Wehrmacht white. Over 1,000 Germans were being killed every day in France and the OKW (Oberkommando der Wehrmacht – the German High Command) nightmare of a war on two Fronts was now a reality. This was actually an understatement of course, as it did not include the Italian Front which, although not of the order of magnitude of Normandy, still required significant German military resources that were sorely needed elsewhere.

As the Germans scrambled to react to the new Front in the west the Soviets seized their chance and thrust forward once more. The Soviet summer offensive, Operation Bagration, was deliberately timed to coincide with the anniversary of the launch of Operation Barbarossa three years previously. The main weight of the offensive fell on the German Army Group Centre, and proceeded to tear it to bloody pieces. Three-quarters of a million German soldiers faced over two million Soviets equipped with an advantage in tanks of over four to one and in artillery of nearly three to one.

As Bagration developed, the huge forces of the 1st Ukrainian and the 1st White Russian Fronts launched a series of coordinated attacks on their massively outnumbered and outgunned opponents of Army Group North Ukraine on 13 July. This German Army Group comprised the grandly named 1st and 4th Panzer Armies, which in reality were nothing like the Panzer Armies of yesteryear. Indeed the 4th Panzer Army in particular had never recovered from its crucifixion the previous year in Kursk, during its so-called 'death ride' against the massed Soviet tank armies.

Panzers were in fact a scarce commodity in the Panzer Armies, the majority of their troops being infantry divisions of much reduced strength with limited heavy weapons. The Soviets by contrast could call on the up-to-strength 1st and 3rd Guards Tank Armies, the 4th Tank Army and a Cavalry-Mechanized Group along with the combined artillery assets of the two engaged Fronts. The result was entirely predictable. The initial offensive resulted in the encirclement and partial destruction of the German XIII Corps within three days of the offensive being launched, followed by a thrust by 1st Guards Tank Army that took Rava Russkaya and separated the 1st and 4th Panzer Armies. The Soviets rushed to exploit the situation and drove deeper into the flanks and rear areas of the German formations, seeking to outflank and encircle as many German units as possible before they could react to try and recover their shattered front lines or counter-attack. Chelm fell to the Soviet advance, and then Lublin fell on 22 July, and the spearheads of the 1st Guards Tank Army reached the banks of the San river near Jaroslaw without sight of any German troops. The gap between the 1st and 4th Panzer Armies was now over thirty miles! The imminent danger was of the encirclement and annihilation of the 4th Panzer Army in particular, unless it could retreat behind the San and Vistula rivers. Any student of Hitler's command of the Eastern Front would consider such a request to be laughable, and unlikely to say the least in light of his 'last man and last bullet' philosophy. However, after a deal of prevarication, permission was actually given on 25 July 1944. It was just too late. The Soviets had already seized bridgeheads across both the San and the Vistula and were fanning out to the west. OKW activated the 17th Army in response and allocated an initial pitiful two-and-a-half divisions, that were then built up to five divisions by 31 July, in order to provide the counter-offensive force that was designed to wipe out the Soviet bridgeheads and throw the Red Army back behind the San and

Vistula rivers. At this time the Soviets were weakened after carrying out a major break-in battle, a series of meeting engagements, lightning advances and two large-scale river crossings. Their supply lines were fully extended and both troops and equipment needed a refit.

German counter-offensive

The German counter-offensive launched on 31 July, by both the 17th Army and 4th Panzer Army, sought to exploit that situation but petered out in the face of fierce Soviet resistance after only two days. Little more than a week after the failure of the German counter-blow the Soviets renewed their offensive. Although not of the proportions of the July attacks it still made headway against the weak German forces facing it and a series of towns including Krosno fell to the Soviets. Reinforcements were desperately needed to try and shore up the crumbling front and it was into this maelstrom that the SS-Sturmbrigade Frankreich was thrown for its baptism of blood and fire.

1,000 Frenchmen against the tide

The Brigade as a whole was not in any state to be deployed operationally with the 2nd Battalion only just beginning to form, so the decision was made to concentrate everyone who was considered combat ready into a reinforced 1st Battalion under Waffen-Hauptsturmführer Pierre Cance, while the 2nd Battalion continued to form and train. The 36-year-old Cance, like his SS-Sturmbrigade comrade Fenet, was a former Milicien and one of Darnard's right hand men. A native of Bordeaux, he had played rugby for France at international level and won the Croix de Guerre as a reserve infantry lieutenant in the First World War. Commissioned from Bad Tölz in the first batch of French candidates for the Waffen-SS, he was a natural choice to lead the battalion, being a man of huge energy and respected by all. Following the deployment decision the 1st Battalion left its barracks in Neweklau and marched to the embarkation station at Beneschau on 29 July 1944. The following day the French Waffen-SS boarded their troop train and headed east. There is some debate as to the actual combat strength deployed, but a figure of some twenty officers and 980 NCOs and other ranks is considered accurate.

One thousand Frenchmen had had just a few months' training and very little in the way of heavy weapons; one thousand Frenchmen with no panzers, armoured cars and very little transport; one thousand Frenchmen to battle the Red tide; one thousand Frenchmen at a time when entire German divisions were being wiped off the map by the steamrolling offensive of the Red Army. And yet from this seemingly doomed, and impossibly gallant, group would come the men who would form the hard wood of Charlemagne in 1945. The men whose names would come to dominate Charlemagne's combat diary in Pomerania, and who would lead her in the final conflagration in Berlin, were there in Galicia at the beginning. The names of Henri Fenet, André Bayle, Henri Kreis, François Appolot, Eugène Vaulot, Jean Croisille and Yvan Bartolomei began to be heard in Galicia, and would continue to be heard until the end. Others would add their names to the Charlemagne roster of honour during the later battles. Men such as Pierre Rostaing, Michel de Genouillac and Emile Raybaud, but it was those 1,000 Frenchmen slowly heading east on their Deutsche Reichsbahn train in the hot summer of 1944 who would begin the French Waffen-SS story, and to a large extent it would be the same men who would finish it less than a year later.

The train journey took a week, and at the end on 5 August the Frenchmen disembarked in the town of Turka, and began the march to their deployment positions. That march was east to a large town called Sanok. The plan was for them to marry up there with the division they had been attached to. This was SS-Oberführer Wilhelm Trabandt's 18th SS-Freiwilligen-Panzer-Grenadier Division Horst Wessel, which was positioned on the rail lines running towards the old Polish royal city of Cracow. The Horst Wessel was a new Division itself, only being raised in 1944, and as its nomenclature of 'Freiwilligen' denoted it was a Volksdeutsche unit.

Based on an experienced cadre of German personnel, the unit was filled with volunteers from Hungary's large racial German population. Although some of the Volksdeutsche units were dubious in terms of their military value, there was no doubt that Horst Wessel was an excellent division of first-rate fighting quality, and it was extremely keen to bring the Frenchmen into the line as it desperately needed reinforcements. Indeed Trabandt even sent back a column of trucks to pick up the Frenchmen and rush them forward. He then met Cance and his officers on the night of 8 August and explained that the situation was deteriorating rapidly. The majority of the Horst Wessel was just about holding its own, but on his Division's left flank he had deployed a regimental-sized grouping based on his SS Panzer Grenadier Regiment 40, commanded by the Knight's Cross holder, SS-Sturmbannführer Ernst Schäfer. This unit, designated SS-Kampfgruppe Schäfer, was struggling unsuccessfully to seal off the huge hole torn in the Wehrmacht's front by the Soviets on the Horst Wessel's left flank. The Kampfgruppe was meant to be of the size of a British brigade, some 2,500 men, but savage fighting had reduced the strength of its fighting companies down to as few as twenty-five men each.

The French battalion was immediately pressed into action to help seal off the gap, with Fenet's 3rd Company being the first into action. Linking up with SS-Untersturmführer Tämpfer's twenty-man company of the

Horst Wessel on the extreme left of the German line, Fenet's men clashed with a nest of Red Army snipers in a hamlet on 9 August, and section commander Sturmmann Delattre of the 1st Platoon was killed. He was the first French Waffen-SS man from the SS-Sturmbrigade Frankreich to be killed in action. He would definitely not be the last.

The 2nd Company under its commander, Léon Gaultier, was next into action. Gaultier was 29 years old and a history teacher by profession, from Berry, a pre-war member of Doriot's PPF who had volunteered to fight the communist threat. His Company came under heavy fire and received a bloody nose trying to capture the forest of Dundynce. 2nd Company's baptism of fire was swiftly followed by Nöel de Tissot leading his 1st Company up in support of the attack of the mauled 2nd Company. De Tissot was 30 years old and a native of Nice. Like Gaultier he was a teacher by profession, a maths teacher this time, who had fought as a reservist NCO against the Germans in 1939 to 1940. He was also a member of the PPF, but an ardent supporter of Darnard as well. De Tissot joined the SOL, then the Milice, before volunteering for the Waffen-SS at Darnard's urging.

The SS-Sturmbrigade's first full day of combat on 10 August was a tough one. About twenty volunteers were killed, but much more worrying than the total number killed was the fact that it was the SS-Sturmbrigade's commanders who were falling. Out of action on that first day were one company commander, six platoon commanders and some twenty section commanders. This loss of junior leaders was common among Waffen-SS units where leadership from the front was highly prized, but the effect was to quickly lessen the military impact of a unit unless it had a steady stream of replacement commanders; this the SS-Sturmbrigade would not get. As an example the 1st Platoon of the 1st Company lost its platoon commander wounded, the 24-year-old Waffen-Untersturmführer Paul Pignard-Berthet, and all its three section commanders, Atama, Cran and Jacqot. Without its leaders the entire 1st Platoon was headless and of limited military value. Haemorrhaging of its commanders on this scale could not be sustained for long.

Mielec and Kreis at Radomysl

Over the next week the SS-Sturmbrigade was constantly in and out of action in a bitter, infantry dominated battle. Gradually the Front settled, and the fighting at Sanok died down as the pocket was sealed. The Frenchmen had fought well, but had suffered over 100 casualties already. The decision was then made to send the remaining French SS men to a sector that was in sore need of reinforcement. A column of trucks was found and the unit was transferred to Mielec, a town about 100 kilometres northwest of Sanok. This transfer was standard practice for Waffen-SS units on the Eastern Front. Wherever the action was the hardest that was where the Führer's fire brigades of the Waffen-SS were sent. In this new sector, on Sunday 20 August at 0700hrs Pierre Cance received a telephone call from his old commander, Sturmbannführer Schäfer, whose Kampfgruppe had been moved as well. Schäfer was blunt: 'Tanks have broken through to the north-east. Send your anti-tank platoon at once to Radomysl.'

Radomysl was a village behind the main French positions, and if it fell they would effectively be cut off from any retreat. Waffen-Oberjunker (officer candidate), Henri Kreis (whose *nom de guerre* was Henri Kreutzer) took his three anti-tank PAK guns and his thirty men, and arrived in the town at 0900hrs, with orders to hold it until 1600hrs that afternoon, or die trying. Kreis himself was already considered an international Waffen-SS classic, only 19 years old but tall, blond, energetic and a natural leader. He was very athletic, and was the holder of the European hand grenade throwing record, at 70 metres, from his time at Bad Tölz. At the time the hand grenade throw was considered a military sport.

On their arrival Kreis positioned his own men facing the anticipated Soviet advance from the east, and then set about scavenging everything he could to strengthen his meagre command. He corralled another seventy or so German stragglers together, and more importantly a Sturmgeschütz self-propelled gun, to bolster the thin defence line. It was just in time; at midday the Russian wave hit. Kreis and his 100 men were attacked by an entire Soviet infantry regiment with tank support. The first assault was stopped in a hail of automatic gunfire, but as ever the Russians were undaunted and pressed home attack after attack. The Soviet infantry, though brave, were unable to break through the wall of fire put up by the defenders, and so tanks were committed to the battle. Kreis's gun crews and the Sturmgeschütz were supplemented by the panzerfäusts of their infantry comrades as they fought to hold back the Russian tanks. Tank after tank was hit by the French and German fire but the Russians would not be denied and pressed home their assault. The fighting became house-to-house until eventually Kreis concentrated his remaining men and last two guns in the village cemetery to make a final stand. The fighting was savage, with Kreis himself being badly wounded as he personally destroyed a Soviet tank with a panzerfäust, but they held as ordered until relieved at 1900hrs that night. Kreis was then evacuated to hospital in Vienna and awarded the Iron Cross 1st Class for his leadership at Radomysl.

Battle at Mokré

As Kreis and his platoon were fighting madly in the dust and blood of Radomysl the rest of the SS-Sturmbrigade came under heavy attack from a fresh Soviet offensive which saw the Frenchmen pulled back pell-mell from the Visloka river line down to the south-east, to concentrate on the town of Mokré.

The withdrawal was chaotic, with retreating Frenchmen and Germans becoming hopelessly mixed up and lost. Waffen-Standartenoberjunker (officer candidate), Abel Chapy, had taken over the 1st Platoon of 1st Company from the wounded Pignard-Berthet, and now his reduced platoon played a vital role in fighting a desperate rearguard action while the rest of the French SS men slowly regrouped in Mokré. No sooner had Cance established a makeshift defence on the night of 21 August, than the Russian attacks began again. The fighting continued to rage all day on the 22nd and into the night. Just as in Radomysl, the French troopers held their ground, but again as in Radomysl the Russians were not to be denied their victory and continued to press home attack after attack. One by one the French volunteers went down, Cance himself being wounded three times in the fighting. The Frenchmen held throughout the day, but shortage of ammunition soon became a serious issue, particularly as the panzerfäusts ran out and the Russian tanks kept coming. Ordered to hold out for a further twelve hours the fighting grew in a crescendo and the French casualties mounted. The French casualty list included the 2nd Company's commander, Robert Lambert, platoon commander Le Marquer and the SS-Sturmbrigade's own German Liaison officer, SS-Untersturmführer Hans Reiche, who was blown to pieces in a direct artillery hit on the battalion HQ.

The French held for the twelve hours, but finally the pressure told and the few remaining SS men were violently bundled out of Mokré. Sadly many of the more seriously wounded Frenchmen couldn't flee with their comrades and were killed by the Russians in the final assault. The resultant retreat was even more frantic than the earlier one from the Visloka, with the surviving Frenchmen having to fight a series of running engagements with the advancing Russians. By now unwounded French SS officers were rarer than unicorns, with Waffen-Untersturmführer Maudy being the only surviving, unwounded platoon commander, and overall command of the SS-Sturmbrigade falling to the near-50-year-old Waffen-Obersturmführer Jean Croisille, who had two sons serving with the SS-Sturmbrigade. Unbeknown to the ever cheerful Croisille, one of his sons had been killed in Mokré. The retreating Frenchmen found some available transport and headed west putting as much distance between themselves and the still advancing Soviets as possible. Finally the French convoy reached the town of Tarnow and relative safety, and it was here that they could now count the cost of a fortnight of vicious combat against a foe that outnumbered and outgunned them at all times.

Of the 1,000 Frenchmen who began the Galician battles, seven officers and 130 other ranks were killed, eight officers and 661 men were wounded and forty men were missing. This then meant that fifteen out of the original twenty officers and 831 out of 980 other ranks were casualties. This was a grand total of 846 from the original 1,000 men as casualties. Even by the shocking standards of the Eastern Front this was bloodletting on a horrendous scale. A single fortnight's combat had shattered a formation it had taken the best part of a year to establish, recruit, train and equip. There was still the uncommitted 2nd Battalion back in Germany, and quite a few individuals away on various specialist training courses, and many of those who were wounded would return to active service fairly quickly, but this could not hide the fact that the SS-Sturmbrigade Frankreich had fought itself to near extinction in trying to hold up Operation Bagration on the plains and rivers of Galicia.

However, just like their comrades in the LVF, the Frenchmen of the SS-Sturmbrigade had now proved themselves in combat and earned themselves a citation on 24 August in the Divisional Orders of Horst Wessel, and the personal praise of SS-Oberführer Trabandt. Trabandt even turned up on the 28th at the SS-Sturmbrigade's camp near Tarnow and distributed a total of fifty-eight Iron Crosses, many to the surviving 150 men on parade, but an equally high number, twenty-nine in fact, as posthumous awards. Among the recipients were Pierre Cance (wounded), Henri Kreis (wounded), Robert Lambert (dead), Marc Godillon and Emilien Boyer (an ex-Milicien who was shot after the war for his Milice activity).

Leaving Galicia

On 1 September 1944 the survivors boarded a train at Tarnow railway station and headed west for their new home at Wildflecken camp in the old Danzig Corridor in northern Germany. It was almost a month to the day since they had first boarded a train at Beneschau to take them to the Eastern Front, and here they were heading back west to an uncertain future.

Galicia was a hard training ground for the French SS men, and one from which so many of the eager volunteers did not return, but they had fought well and learnt the vital lessons that all front-line units must learn if they are not to disintegrate when in combat. Now the survivors could lick their wounds, and head to Wildflecken camp to be reunited with their comrades of the 2nd Battalion, and the many and varied Frenchmen who were being brought from all over the Third Reich to form the newly-established Charlemagne Division. As such these now veteran Frenchmen of the SS-Sturmbrigade would join their fellow countrymen of the LVF as the hard core of the new Division in some of the final battles of the Second World War. Both the LVF and the SS-Sturmbrigade Frankreich had now had their hallmark battles; the LVF at the Bobr river and the SS-Sturmbrigade at Mokré. Both units would need the inspiration from those battles, as 1945 dawned with the coming of the Charlemagne.

Names to remember

Pierre Rostaing had, of course, taken no part in the Galician battles as he was in the LVF at the time. But even so 1944 had been a momentous year for him so far. He had seen his second consecutive year of active service on the Russian Front, been decorated for bravery on several occasions and had taken part in the bloodshed on the Bobr. He had also seen his unit prepared for disbandment, and seen a new breed of French volunteer on arrival at Wildflecken. These were not the casually dressed, relaxed, but fiercely 'French legionnaires' of the LVF, but hard, disciplined young men, proud of their status as Europeans, and very definitely Waffen-SS in ethos, tone and appearance. Rostaing was not one of them, but he fitted right in. The Waffen-SS ideal of excellence in the profession of arms spoke to Rostaing's soul; this was his calling and he knew it. He was still very much a 'soldier of France', but he would nevertheless be at home in the Waffen-SS.

For Henri Fenet it had been an earthquake of a year. In 1943 he had been a Milicien commander down in Ain, skirmishing with local, lightly armed *résistants*. In 1944 he had started the year by attending a special officer training course conducted specifically for French candidates, *Nr.1 Sonderlehrgang für französische Offiziere*, at the famed Bad Tölz academy, along with twenty-three fellow French officer candidates. The intake included Pierre Cance, Jean Croisille, Abel Chapy, Léon Gaultier, Henri Kreis, Paul Pignard-Berthet and Noel de Tissot among others, with the course running from 10 January to 4 March. On graduation Henri Fenet was commissioned as a Waffen-Obersturmführer (full lieutenant), and took command of the 3rd Company of the SS-Sturmbrigade's 1st Battalion in April 1944. Pushing his new company hard, he had almost been killed accidentally in a trademark live firing exercise on the training grounds at Neweklau. His fellow Bad Tölz graduate, Waffen-Oberjunker Henri Kreis, led an attack on his command post and a stray bullet went through the death's head emblem on Fenet's cap!

As Operation Bagration struck the Germans in the East, Fenet was confirmed as the commander of the 3rd Company in the battalion being sent to the Front at Sanok in Galicia. On arrival at the Front, it was Fenet's 3rd Company that was the first into action and it was one of his men, the previously mentioned Sturmmann Delattre who became the SS-Sturmbrigade's first fatality. On transfer to the Mielec sector, Fenet and his company found themselves holding a stretch of the line including the village of Pouby on the night of 20–21 August. As they dug in, they were hit by an entire Soviet Guards infantry battalion attack supported by mortars and anti-tank guns. The fighting was savage and often hand to hand. Attack after attack came in and the company was ground to pieces. Quicampoix's 1st Platoon fell back in confusion, Couvreur's 4th Heavy Platoon was scattered, and

Laschett's 2nd Platoon was encircled and forced to surrender when their ammo ran out. Waffen-Oberjunker Charles Laschett would later die in the Soviet gulag at Tambov in early 1945. By midday on the 21st it was all over. Fenet gathered his remaining fifty men and fell back in an attempt to reach Mokré and the rest of the battalion. Fighting all the way, Fenet managed somehow to get his battered company back to Mokré, on the way supporting Chapy's desperate rearguard action and rescuing the battalion HQ staff from attack. At Mokré, during the hurried reorganisation of the battalion, he was separated from his company and ended up commanding a scratch force of Army, German Waffen-SS and military police personnel fighting around the town of Debica. He was wounded by shrapnel in the shoulder and evacuated. When SS-Oberführer Trabandt came to present the awards to the SS-Sturmbrigade at the end of August on his list was an Iron Cross 1st Class for Waffen-Obersturmführer Henri Fenet.

As for the incredibly young André Bayle, Galicia was an experience that changed his life for ever. He had not served in the pre-war French Army, and had seen very little of the Blitzkrieg of the summer of 1940. Since then he had eagerly kept abreast of all the news from the war, particularly from the Eastern Front, but had played no direct part. Galicia was to change all that. As a Waffen-Unterscharführer (junior/lance sergeant), André Bayle was in the 2nd Platoon of Léon Gaultier's 2nd Company. The 2nd Company was hit hard in the initial fighting, and was then tasked with attacking and clearing the village of Pisarowce some kilometres from the rest of the battalion.

Waffen-Oberjunker Joseph Peyron was the Platoon Commander, and he led the platoon on a night march to rendezvous with a troop of German panzers who were to support his attack on the village the next morning. On reaching the village at daybreak, after a long and tiring route march, Peyron went forward to recce the village and see if the Russians were still in possession of it. They were, in fact the place was crawling with them! So many in fact that they stormed out and encircled the forty men of the 2nd Platoon in a cornfield. The tired and footsore SS grenadiers had no choice, to stay was to die, so they fixed bayonets and charged. The Russians poured fire into the running Frenchmen, but the charge didn't falter, even when Peyron went down under the blast of a mortar round. Bayle was now the platoon commander, and he urged his men on as they stormed from house to house in the village cutting down every Russian soldier in sight. Pisarowce was soon in SS hands, but only twenty-five members of the platoon were left alive. It was then that the promised panzer support arrived, and so impressed was their commanding officer that he immediately proposed the 17-year-old Bayle for the Iron Cross 2nd Class. Bayle then led the remains of his platoon back to rejoin the battalion, and went to their new sector at Mielec on the Visloka river.

Robert Lambert now commanded 2nd Company, replacing the wounded Léon Gaultier, as it sat on the river line facing a seemingly quiet enemy. The peace was a charade; on the flanks of the SS-Sturmbrigade the Russians caved in the neighbouring German units, and almost without warning on the evening of 20 August the Frenchmen found themselves surrounded. The SS-Sturmbrigade prepared to break out west to a new position based on Mokré. 2nd Company was to lead, but as it began to withdraw it ran into heavy Russian opposition and was caught in a bitter fire fight. Trying to move and fight at the same time the company splintered. Bayle found himself with fifteen survivors whom he managed to disengage from the Soviet pursuit, and they headed for Mokré. In the same break-out battle, Abel Chapy somehow got the majority of 1st Company out and back to Mokré, while Fenet's 3rd Company was ripped apart. In the meantime Bayle threaded his small command through the hordes of advancing Soviets. After a nerve-wracking night avoiding Russian patrols they marched into Mokré in the morning and rejoined their comrades. They were a desperately needed reinforcement for the hard-pressed grenadiers.

Bayle was then fully involved in the bloodbath of Mokré. Here, he and the other French SS men fought tooth and nail to keep the Russians out of the burning village. The Soviets took the place, house by house, killing every SS man they found, until the last defenders were grouped at the farmhouse and courtyard that was serving as battalion headquarters. Everywhere there were wounded Frenchmen lying on the ground, but when the time came to abandon the position, there was no opportunity to take them with the survivors, and most died in the final Russian onslaught. Bayle survived the butchery, and after the battle back in Tarnow, he received his Iron Cross from SS-Oberführer Trabandt personally.

Rough Justice

As a postscript to the fighting in Galicia the SS-Sturmbrigade lost one of its most able and dedicated leaders, Waffen-Oberjunker Abel Chapy. Chapy was a fierce French nationalist, and a national socialist, who had served in both the Spahis and the Chasseurs d'Afrique before the war. He missed the German invasion and was then demobilised as an Aspirant, returning home to Tours in 1941. He dallied with the SOL, Déat's RNP, Deloncle's MSR and the Phalange Africaine before joining the Milice and training at Uriage. He then went over to the Waffen-SS and attended Bad Tölz along with Fenet and the rest of the French SS contingent.

Chapy was dynamic and determined, and this came to the fore in the Galician battles where he soon took over command of the 1st Company when de Tissot was wounded. During the chaotic retreat to Mokré, he had led his company in a desperate rearguard action to allow the rest of the SS-Sturmbrigade to escape. He had then continued to lead a hotchpotch of men from the smashed 1st and 3rd Companies in the fighting near Debica; indeed Fenet must have been close to this action. Though wounded, Chapy had refused to be evacuated, and on the unit being withdrawn to Tarnow, he was confirmed as commander of the 3rd Company.

However, once at Tarnow, and awaiting orders to entrain for Wildflecken, Chapy grew increasingly incensed with the actions of the Verwaltung, the Supply Corps. Like so many front-line soldiers before and since, Chapy considered rear area soldiers like the Supply Corps with barely concealed contempt. Chapy's particular *bête noire* was a certain SS-Unterscharführer Egle, an Alsatian, whom Chapy suspected of stealing the belongings of the dead and wounded. Chapy warned Egle about his behaviour, but was then given evidence that he had refused to carry a wounded French comrade to a first aid post during the recent battles. This was too much for Chapy who accused Egle of cowardice, in front of several witnesses, and then executed him on the spot. Having killed him, Chapy buried him and told several officers, including Criosille, what he had done. No one had a clue what to do. However the truth came out and Chapy was arrested and sent to the military prison in Cracow. Months later he was tried by a court from the Wallonian SS Division of all things, found guilty and sent to Dachau. The situation actually came to Himmler's attention, and the Reichsführer duly overturned the verdict and returned Chapy to service immediately. Too late to join his comrades of the Charlemagne, in Germany's growing chaos, Chapy joined the nearest fighting formation he could find, and ended up fighting the Americans as they fought across Germany. On his return to France at the end of the war he was arrested and imprisoned for his war service in the Waffen-SS.

CHAPTER VIII

A New Beginning: The Formation of Charlemagne

Whilst the 1st Battalion of the SS-Sturmbrigade Frankreich was still fighting for its life in Galicia, the decision was made by Reichsführer-SS Heinrich Himmler to merge all existing French armed servicemen into a new formation. The official launch was on 10 August 1944 when the SS Main Office ordered the formation of the newly-titled Waffen-Grenadier-Brigade der SS Charlemagne (franz. Nr.1). Oberst Edgar Puaud, commander of the LVF, was given command of the new brigade and promoted to Waffen-Oberführer. This then was the birth of Charlemagne, and though the unit would go through a series of re-designations and names, so common in the Waffen-SS, this was the unit that would emerge as the 33rd Waffen-Grenadier-Division der SS Charlemagne (französische Nr.1), fight its inaugural battles in Pomerania, and be almost wiped out in Berlin.

The decision to create the new formation was taken in light of the heavy fighting of the Soviet 1944 summer offensive. Both the LVF and the SS-Sturmbrigade Frankreich were now accepted by Himmler and the Nazi High Command as battle-proven formations after Bobr and Mokré, but their casualties had been such that it was obvious an amalgamation was needed to use the remaining French volunteers most effectively. So a formation was to be created into which all the remaining Frenchmen serving with the Germans would be combined. At Himmler's insistence this new formation was to be an SS one. This was a huge shift in official Nazi policy but the reality of the military situation necessitated much in the way of forgetting outmoded racial fantasies. So why the name Charlemagne, and what would the new unit look like?

Charles the Frank as a pan-Germanic hero

As for the honour title of 'Charlemagne', even at this late stage of the war it was a matter of heated and protracted debate. Whereas the German

Army used honour titles sparingly, and then usually only for their elite divisions, such as the Grossdeutschland and Feldherrnhalle, the Waffen-SS used them much more often but the honorifics had huge symbolism and were the subject of often heated debate at senior level within the SS. However, there was a certain lack of reasoning in the system. Honour titles were originally intended to mark units out in recognition of an illustrious pedigree or distinguished service, but this was not always the case. For instance Himmler bestowed honour titles on the Croatian and Bosnian Muslim SS divisions, the 13th Handschar and 23rd Kama, when their service records were truly abysmal. These Divisions excelled only in the murder of civilians, and were a military embarrassment. Indeed the Handschar was remarkable in that it was the only Waffen-SS unit ever to mutiny! Whereas the three Waffen-SS divisions raised from the Baltic countries of Latvia, Lithuania and Estonia, the 15th, 19th and 20th SS divisions, were of a very high calibre with excellent combat records, and yet none were given honour titles.

Himmler took the view that the past performance of both the LVF and the SS-Sturmbrigade Frankreich entitled the new unit to be given its own honour title – but what?

As ever with the symbols involved in military life the subject was the topic of endless debate and discussion and an issue of great importance. It has been ever so and remains today; for confirmation one need only read the newspaper columns whenever yet another reorganisation of the British Army threatens to extinguish a revered regimental name!

A range of titles were discussed and summarily rejected until only two options remained: that of 'Joan of Arc' (in French, Jeanne d'Arc) and 'Charlemagne' (in German, Karl der Grosse). The former was very much the choice of Darnard and his Miliciens, representing as they saw it a strongly nationalist, avowedly Catholic heroine and saviour of the French people. These reasons were precisely why Himmler objected to the Maid; for him Joan of Arc was too narrowly French and nationalistic. The Albanians of the 21st SS division may have been able to have their national hero, Iskander Beg (Skanderbeg was the chosen derivative), as their honour title but that was different in Himmler's view because Skanderbeg's achievement was to expel Albania's eastern Moslem conquerors, an act that fitted entirely with the Reichsführer's world view. Joan of Arc did no such thing, indeed the racial enemy she fought were the Anglo-Saxon English who were definitely brother Aryans in Himmler's twisted world view. The Frankish king-emperor Charlemagne was much more to Himmler's liking. Originally used as a temporary title for the Reichsdeutsche 9th SS Panzer Division during its formation in 1943, that unit was then awarded the honour title of Frundsberg and thus Charlemagne was 'going spare' as it were.

Why did Himmler favour Charlemagne? Firstly, he was one of the Frankish Carolingian kings who ruled over most of modern-day France and parts of western Germany. The Franks themselves were a Germanic people who had settled in Gaul under their leader Clovis during the breakdown of the 'old' Roman Empire. In AD 800, in one of history's ironies, Clovis's successor, Charlemagne, was crowned Emperor of the 'new' Holy Roman Empire. He led campaigns against the Moslem rulers of Moorish Spain and the pagan Slavic Avars in the east. These achievements and his unification of German and French culture also contributed to Himmler's benign feelings towards him. However, he also led a vicious campaign to convert the pagan Saxons to Christianity and in one barbarous episode executed some 4,500 Saxon men, women and children on a single day in AD 782. This avowedly anti-pagan and anti-Saxon side to his career excluded Charlemagne from the pantheon of true Germanic heroes, as far as Himmler was concerned, but he was seen as the best of a bad lot and therefore adopted. The die was cast and Germany's French SS men were from then on to be inextricably linked with the name of 'Charlemagne'.

Having decided on its name what was the new Charlemagne Division to look like? Was it to be an armoured formation, or infantry, and how large would it be? In the Germany of late 1944 there was no real choice in terms of weaponry available; the German armaments industry was reeling under round the clock bombing by both RAF Bomber Command and the 8th USAAF, and combined with a lack of raw materials Germany could not properly equip her existing panzer formations let alone establish new ones. Charlemagne would then be an infantry formation. In terms of her projected size, the terrible attrition rates the composite elements of Charlemagne had suffered in the East meant that it was sensible to initially keep her to a 'brigade' status, in case the numbers volunteering didn't merit the establishment of a true division. During this transitional time the unit was variously entitled the Französische Brigade der SS and the Waffen-Grenadier Brigade der SS 'Charlemagne' (französische Nr.1) among others. During this phase the brigade's initial orbat was based on two grenadier regiments and basic supporting elements, as follows:

Stab der Brigade (Headquarters)
- Waffen-Grenadier Regiment der SS 57
- Waffen-Grenadier Regiment der SS 58
- Waffen-Artillerie-Abteilung der SS 57
- SS-Pionieer-Kompanie 57
- SS-Panzerjager-Abteilung 57
- SS-Nachrichten-Kompanie 57

However, finally, on 1 September 1944 at the SS NCO School at Greifenberg in West Prussia, the Charlemagne was officially designated as a Division, combining all the various contingents including the SS-Sturmbrigade and the LVF. The next practical step was the physical formation of the new Division. Although even then there would be more administrative juggling, so that it wasn't until 2 February 1945 that the Division was established formally as 33rd Waffen-Grenadier-Division der SS Charlemagne (französische Nr.1). The Frenchmen were given the divisional number of 33 after the fledgling Hungarian Volksdeutsche unit, originally given the designation, the Waffen-Kavallerie-Division der SS (ungarnische Nr. 4) was annihilated by the Soviets before it had even been properly constituted.

Based on the existing teeth arm, the fighting, elements of two grenadier regiments, numbered respectively 57 and 58, each regiment was to comprise only two grenadier battalions, making the Division small by classic Wehrmacht standards, but in 1945 it was about average for the size of the shrinking Nazi field formations. To beef up the Division's combat power there was to be a fifth grenadier battalion, designated as an assault battalion, initially called the Sturm-Battailon. This unit was to be manned by volunteers from within the Division's ranks, and was to be trained and equipped as an elite within Charlemagne. This battalion never properly materialised, an honour guard unit was created, and this became the Compagnie d'Honneur, but it was never more than a strong company in size. This elite sub-unit would then transform itself again into the Kampfschule, Close Combat School, for its final showdown in Berlin. The Division was to have a range of supporting sub-units, the most important of which were to be one battalion each of artillery and anti-tank heavy weapons, there would also be pioneer and signals companies. The new Division's order of battle was as follows:

SS-Waffen-Grenadier-Regiment 57
* I./SS-Waffen-Grenadier-Regiment 57
* II./SS-Waffen-Grenadier-Regiment 57

SS-Waffen-Grenadier-Regiment 58
* I./SS-Waffen-Grenadier-Regiment 58
* II./SS-Waffen-Grenadier-Regiment 58
* SS-Sturm-Bataillon 58
* SS-Artillerie-Abteilung 33
* SS-Panzerjäger-Abteilung 33
* SS-Pionier-Kompanie 33
* SS-Nachrichten-Kompanie 33
* SS-Feldersatz-Kompanie 33
* SS-Nachschub-Bataillon 33

The importance of the heavy weapons sub-units cannot be overestimated. The war in the East, where undoubtedly the new Division would fight, was one of movement and firepower. Charlemagne lacked mobility, but that handicap could be lessened by the application of large doses of firepower. The mass of Soviet armour could only be successfully met by other armour, or by strong anti-tank elements, and the overwhelming Soviet manpower advantage required artillery to combat it, particularly as the Soviets were liberally supported by their own massed guns. Without these key support units the SS grenadiers of Charlemagne would be woefully unprepared to stand against the Red Army juggernaut as their lightly armed infantry battalions would be ground to bloody shreds by massed Soviet artillery and armour, backed up by huge swarms of Red infantry. However, even with the integral artillery, anti-tank and assault battalions the Charlemagne was in essence a static infantry-heavy unit that was not equipped or configured for anything other than defensive operations. Even then the Division's combat power was not strong with only five infantry battalions to its name, and as Galicia proved for the SS-Sturmbrigade Frankreich, even a short period of fighting on the Eastern Front caused enormous attrition of men very quickly. With little hope of significant reinforcement it was obvious from the birth of Charlemagne that it was a one-shot weapon, one significant battle and it would need to be withdrawn to be reformed and reinforced, and that needed time to accomplish. And in 1945, time was a luxury that the Charlemagne did not have.

The pooling of Hitler's Frenchmen

Through late 1943 and early 1944 there was a steady erosion of Waffen-SS elitism in terms of both racial, physical and ideological standards. This must have seemed dire to many of the early Waffen-SS purists, but it was only a foretaste of what was to come. June 1944, and the opening of the Normandy Front against the Western Allies, was the death knell for any semblance of Waffen-SS exclusivity. Almost unbelievably conscripts were drafted into the Waffen-SS for the very first time, and the Kriegsmarine and Luftwaffe were trawled for men to be compulsorily transferred over for service in newly-established Waffen-SS divisions, or to reinforce those units shattered on the Eastern and Western Fronts. This policy saw over 5,000 sailors and 40,000 members of the Luftwaffe compulsorily join the black guards. Whole new divisions such as the 9th SS Panzer Division Frundsberg and the 10th SS Panzer Division Hohenstaufen were formed from these drafted men, and amazingly performed extremely well for the remainder of the war. In all about a third of the total number of men who served in the Waffen-SS during the war were either conscripts or compulsory transferees. To cap it all in January 1945 the Heer and Waffen-SS combined their recruiting centres, and with that act the day of the Waffen-SS as the epitome of the Teutonic praetorian was over. Now it was a case of letting anyone and everyone in.

For Charlemagne this lowering of entry criteria saw Nazi bureaucracy and officialdom going into hyperactive drive in a bid to concentrate a whole series of possible manpower pools in one place, with sufficient numbers to form a viable unit. First, and most important to find, was the professional, fighting cadre of the new Division. The new formation would need a hard core of experienced, battle-proven troops. These men would overwhelmingly form the officer and NCO ranks of the unit, and would enable the recruits for the fighting companies to be brought up to standard as quickly as possible. Without them the Division would be in a parlous state, and of dubious combat value. The cadre for the Hitlerjugend Division for example, had been supplied by that most combat tested of Waffen-SS units, the Leibstandarte. The resultant unit went on to carve a legend for itself in the bocage of Normandy, and fight to near extinction at Falaise. If Charlemagne was to have anything like that impact the Division's hard wood would have to be hard indeed.

It was no surprise that the LVF and the SS-Sturmbrigade Frankreich were to provide this vital nucleus. Both these units had been trained well, and had combat experience against the Red Army, including the battle honours of Bobr and Mokré.

The SS-Sturmbrigade's 2nd Battalion was still forming and training during the 1st Battalion's struggle in Galicia, and when judged combat ready it was transferred to the towns of Bruss and Schwarnegast, in the same district as the headquarters of the new Division at the SS NCO School at Greifenberg. It was also to this barracks town that the remnants of the LVF had been brought under their commander Edgar Puaud. Here then was the first mixing of the two separate traditions; the Army men of the LVF, distinctly 'French' in outlook and ethos and proudly nationalist. Next to them the French SS men looked like another species. Imbued with the tenets of national socialism, and completely lacking in the laissez-faire of the legionnaires, it was obvious that the two sets of volunteers would struggle to mesh as a unit, but mesh they must if they were to survive the battles to come. Also brought to the Greifenberg concentration point were Frenchmen who were formerly of the Kriegsmarine, NSKK, Organization Todt and the Luftwaffe. It was here then that the Waffen-SS survivors of the SS-Sturmbrigade Galician battles were sent, small in number but utterly vital in supplementing the LVF to form the combat experienced heart of the proposed new Division.

The major contingents brought together under the banner of the Charlemagne were from five sources in the main. The teeth fighting elements were, of course, based on the remnants of the LVF and the SS-

Sturmbrigade Frankreich. These units contributed about 1,200 men each (of which several hundred were SS veterans of the Galician battles). There were around 1,000 men each from the NSKK (the Nationalsozialistisches Kraftfahrkorps – the National Socialist Motor Transport Corps – basically a supply, mechanical and driving corps), and the Organization Todt (uniformed labour corps), and the largest single contingent was approximately 1,500 men from the Kriegsmarine. Finally, and critically, there were some 1,200 Miliciens. There were other assorted bits and pieces from all over the Third Reich's complicated and diverse structure, so that the grand total of recruits for the Charlemagne Division on formation was some 7,340 personnel. To put this in context the establishment of the famed Totenkopf division was over 19,000, and even the Ukrainian 14th Waffen-Grenadier-Division der SS (ukrainische Nr.1) was over 14,000 men strong. The divisional title was a misnomer, the unit was not big enough to warrant it, but it was entirely normal at the time as the Nazis tried to conjure formations from thin air in an attempt to stave off the by now inevitable defeat.

Regiment 57: SS-Sturmbrigade, Regiment 58: LVF

From the start the eclectic mix of the unit made the process of formation a tough road to travel. As things transpired, Waffen-Grenadier Regiment 57 was founded on former SS-Sturmbrigade Frankreich volunteers, while Waffen-Grenadier Regiment 58 was based on the LVF veterans. This situation led to immediate conflict. The two bodies of men were chalk and cheese. Many of the LVF legionnaires were older, veterans of the fighting from 1941 onwards, proud of their 'Frenchness' and their distinctiveness, and breezily contemptuous of the more mundane aspects of military discipline. To them the former SS-Sturmbrigade men were another breed. They were generally younger, indeed many were still teenagers, and they had been moulded by the Waffen-SS into 'European' soldiers, and not French ones. Their adherence to discipline was rigid, their demeanour was serious and in true Waffen-SS style they were dedicated to the profession of arms.

The two groups had only one real thing in common and that was the experience of combat on the Russian Front. This was crucial. Soldiers can, and will, disagree on everything under the sun, but common operational experience inevitably breeds mutual respect. However, this area of common ground was not shared with another major component of the division, the former Miliciens. None of the Milice had served on the Russian Front in their own right, some had served with the LVF or the SS-Sturmbrigade, but they were now Miliciens no longer. For the dispirited mass of Miliciens gathered at Sigmaringen their only combat experience had been against the *franc tireurs* of the Resistance back in the familiar surroundings and lush greenness of their native France. The Miliciens had no Bobr or Mokré to inspire them and give them common ground with the old hares of the LVF or the youthful converts of the SS-Sturmbrigade. After they had been forced to flee France and take refuge in Sigmaringen, Darnard had fought tooth and nail to maintain the Miliciens' independence. While happy to see some of his men, such as Fenet, join the SS-Sturmbrigade Frankreich in order to influence it, he did not want his Milice to be submerged into such an organisation. He attempted to negotiate with the Germans to preserve the separate identity of the Milice and its exclusively 'French' outlook. He was not interested in seeing all of his Milice fighting the hordes from the East when in his view there were enemies enough at home in France. These efforts were ultimately in vain and a self-delusion. The plans drawn up by Darnard and his lieutenants for a counter-attack back into France were pure fantasy, and it was only a matter of time before Darnard and his Milice would have to face the reality of their situation. That reality was that if Germany fell, so did they. They had tied their banner to the swastika and now they were stuck with it to the bitter end. The Miliciens would not even be concentrated in a distinctively Milice regiment as the 57th was ex-SS-Sturmbrigade and the 58th ex-LVF. The paramilitaries of the Milice were dispersed among the two grenadier regiments to ensure they had a cadre of battle hardened soldiers around them. Thus 15% of the Regiment der SS 58 were ex-Miliciens, with the proportion being a fair way higher in Regiment der SS 57. They were also fairly late to the scene, not even arriving at the new depot at Wildflecken until 5 November 1944.

From Greifenberg to Wildflecken

In late 1944 these assorted composite elements were moved from Greifenberg in the east and transported for training at Wildflecken camp, north-west of Frankfurt-am-Main in central Germany. At Wildflecken, the Frenchmen were assembled, sorted and assigned to the Division's various component sub-units, and began serious training. Having carried out initial organisation and restructuring with the ex-LVF, SS-Sturmbrigade, Todt, NSKK and Kriegsmarine men at Greifenberg in the east, here at Wildflecken they would continue and complete their training and be prepared for the Front.

It is difficult to picture the scene at Wildflecken as this truly diverse mix of Frenchmen involved in the German cause came together for the first time. It could be suggested on a simplistic level that their nationality was the source of a common bond between the Frenchmen in the camp but this would be a total misreading of the reality. The component contingents did not have much in common at all beyond their country of origin. They may all have been Frenchmen but they had very different motivations, different experiences, training, leadership and expectations. Trying to establish and build a new formation at any time is a difficult undertaking, but to attempt to do so in the circumstances as they were at the time made the whole process immeasurably harder. To add to the challenge there was the all too obvious beginnings of the inexorable slide towards the final chaos of defeat in Nazi Germany. Only the most militarily naïve individual must have still thought the war was winnable for the German cause; the priority now was to try to stave off the Russian bulldozer for as long as possible.

This motivation to sacrifice everything if necessary in order to frustrate the Soviet juggernaut was immensely powerful towards the end of the war. Nowadays, with general war in Europe a distant memory, and with the final defeat and death of Soviet communism having been accomplished over a decade ago, with Europe, including Eastern Europe, standing free and democratic, it is incredibly difficult to imagine why such a sacrifice could be judged necessary. In modern times the closest parallel could be construed as the fear felt by some in Europe at the rise of militant Islam. However, whereas Islamic terrorism manifests itself in horrific, but individual, acts of terror, at the time in question the perceived threat from the Red tide was all-pervasive and on an entirely different scale. Therefore a rallying cry to defend a free Europe from a Bolshevik onslaught from the East was a real driver for many at Wildflecken.

The German military machine was still functioning though, and so it was necessary for numbers of men from the Division to attend multiple and various specialist schools and courses all over the Third Reich to prepare them for their roles in Charlemagne:

- Officer candidates went to the SS Officer Academy, Kienschlag, Bohemia-Moravia
- Artillery officers to the SS Artillery School, Beneshcau, Bohemia-Moravia
- NCO candidates to the SS NCO School at Posen-Treskau
- Engineers to the SS Pioneer School, Hradischko, Bohemia-Moravia
- Signallers to the SS Signals School, Sterzing-Vipiteno, South Tyrol
- Mechanics, medics and interpreters to Berlin
- Anti-tank men to Jannowitz, Bohemia-Moravia
- Even drivers of the horse drawn transport were sent to the SS Cavalry School at Göttingen.

The mass of grenadiers stayed at Wildflecken for their training.

Waffen-SS training now kicked in with a vengeance and the 33rd Waffen-Grenadier-Division der SS Charlemagne (französische Nr.1) began to come together as a fighting unit. Perhaps the best way to get the flavour of the atmosphere at Wildflecken is to read the comments of a German eyewitness who was there as an instructor, writing after the war:

I was greeted very casually, and the uniforms also varied greatly from person to person. Uniforms were decorated with German but also French medals, medals earned against us in the First World War or in the western campaign of the Second World War as well as Iron Crosses earned by fighting in our ranks. Colourful scarves were seen. Collars were frequently open, and caps tilted rakishly toward the ear, contrary to regulations. They wore a tricolour patch on the right sleeve, as did we instructors. When I sewed on my tricolored insignia, the SS badge on my collar seemed to become more bearable. Now I felt like a soldier for Europe, no matter how unclear and contradictory my ideas about this might have been. In our view we belonged to a White Guard that would save Europe from the red peril ... The brigade was divided into three groups, followers of the French fascist politician Jacques Doriot, members of the pro-Vichy Milice who fought against the maquis of the Resistance and revered Marshal Pétain, and young Frenchmen who volunteered for the SS because they admired Adolf Hitler as Europe's saviour. The brigade was only fused together by the ceremonial oath of allegiance, in which I took part. It took place on November 12. Originally it was planned for the 11th, but the French leaders protested. November 11 was the 26th anniversary of the conclusion of the armistice of 1918 between Germany and the victorious Allies. The French argued that this date could be interpreted as revenge or ridicule. About 8,000 Frenchmen swore to be fidèle et brave jusqu'à la mort (to be brave and loyal to Adolf Hitler until death) just as the SS song of loyalty demanded: 'We will remain true even if all others abandon you.' This time in Wildflecken was for me the happiest time in this war. Here I got to know people I could converse with. They were open-minded, sensitive, and shaped by the democratic traditions of their country ... There were hardly any peasants among them, also none of the typical bourgeois. On the contrary; the young volunteers were above all rebels against the Philistine attitude (Spießertum) prevalent in France. They loved discussions, elegant phrases, and grand gestures. They questioned all arguments, even their own. I entered a whole new SS reality and was fascinated and confused at the same time. Most of the young French SS volunteers considered themselves a White Guard, part of a great, militant movement against Communism; they considered themselves fighters for a 'new Europe' in which France would be an equal member. They were, to use the terminology of today, fascists with a human face.[1]

This then was Wildflecken, the calm before the inevitable and growing storm gathering in the East.

Note

1. Franz Schönhuber, with the French Volunteers of the Waffen-SS Brigade Charlemagne, date unknown.

Pre-war political rally of far Right extremists in the Velodrome d'Hiver, Paris.

Jacques Doriot: charismatic ex-communist and leader of the main French fascist party, the *Parti Populaire Français* (PPF).

France defeated: the ageing hero of Verdun, Marshal Philippe Pétain, meets the face of the conqueror, Adolf Hitler, at Montoire on 24 October 1940.

The *Milice française* was originally founded in January 1943 as a French nationalist bulwark against anti-Vichy forces, particularly the communists. It soon became a vehicle for collaboration with the Germans. Here is a recruiting poster for Miliciens emphasising the anti-communist nature of the force.

Recruitment poster; while not as sophisticated as some other German graphics of the war period, seen at their best in the brilliantly designed propaganda magazine *Signal*, which was distributed throughout occupied Europe, it has all the usual elements: camaraderie, training, victory.

A training intake at the Milice officer school in Uriage stands at ease. Note the Milice gamma symbol on the wall above the recruits. Many of these men would go on to serve with the Charlemagne.

The result. A trainload of volunteers for the LVF leaves Paris for the training ground at Deba in Poland, 1941.

This propaganda photo shows two LVF legionnaires on the Eastern Front. The one on the left carries the famous MP40 *Schmeisser* machine-pistol, and has the distinctive French tricolour armshield on his top right sleeve with the word 'France' above it.

An award ceremony in Krushina in 1942 for members of the LVF...

…But for many of the legionnaires theirs was a different fate. This cemetery in the village of Smorki, near Borissov, was home to those men from the LVF 1st Battalion who fell fighting the Soviet partisans in 1942 and 1943.

A bemedalled LVF veteran leads his men on parade back home in *la belle France*.

The SS-Sturmbrigade: SS-Untersturmführer Hans Reiche, the German liaision officer serving with the Sturmbrigade in Galicia. He was killed by a shell blast in Mokré on 22nd August 1944.

Seen here from the front cover of the French Waffen-SS propaganda newspaper, *Le Devenir*, from July 1944, from left to right: Hans Reiche, Waffen-Sturmbannführer Paul-Marie Gamory-Dubordeau (Sturmbrigade commander), Waffen-Hauptsturmführer Pierre Cance (led the Sturmbrigade throughout the Galician campaign and was wounded three times at Mokré), SS-Hauptsturmführer 'Koko' Kostenbader (Waffen-SS instructor), and Waffen-Untersturmführer Dominique Scapula (Sturmbrigade orderly officer).

Gare de l'Est, Paris, 6th January 1943, Joseph Darnard (far right) sees off SS-Sturmbrigade volunteers on their way to the Eastern Front.

From left to right: Waffen-Oberjunker Henri Kreis, the battle commander of Radomysl in Galicia, the PPF member Joseph Pleyber, the French nurse Nelly and Dr Bonnefoy.

Officers deliberate over a map, from left to right: Reiche, Ernst Schäffer (commander of SS Regiment 40 of the Horst Wessel) Waffen-Hauptsturmführer Pierre Cance, the ex-beer brewer and seller, and chef de Milice.

Waiting: French SS men await the Red onslaught. Henri Fenet is almost certainly the bespectacled man on the left, the man on the right is wearing the distinctive French SS tricolour armshield on his lower left sleeve.

An SS-Sturmbrigade mortar team in action in Galicia.

An MG42 with its SS-Sturmbrigade crew set up ready for action in Galicia.

Right: SS-Oberführer Wilhelm Trabandt, Commander of the Horst Wessel in Galicia to which the Frenchmen of the SS-Sturmbrigade were attached.

Below: Dr Bonnefoy hands out cigarettes to some of the French SS walking wounded.

A French SS patrol walks by
a dead Soviet soldier.

Badges of the French volunteers:
on the bottom is the tricolour
armshield of the LVF surmounted
by the honour title 'France', and
above the SS armshield.

The conditions in Pomerania were horrendous. The fierce fighting was against a backdrop of freezing temperatures and feet of snow. Here French SS grenadiers of Charlemagne wait in the snow for the next attack, while dead Red Army soldiers lie in front of their guns.

SS grenadiers have to resort to sucking snow for moisture, the supply system long having broken down.

SS-Brigadeführer Dr Gustav Krukenberg: a lawyer by profession, he led Charlemagne during the Pomeranian campaign, and in Berlin he commanded not only the Frenchmen but the whole Nordland division

Above and below: In an infamous incident the Free French commander of the 2nd Armoured Division, General Leclerc, questions the 13 French SS Charlemagne and LVF veterans captured by the Americans and handed over to his men at Bad Reichenhall. The prisoners mocked Leclerc and were promptly executed.

Since the end of the war the Charlemagne veterans have erected a monument to their murdered comrades at Bad Reichenhall.

French SS veterans reunion in Nice, 1990 – from left to right: Pierre Rostaing (the most decorated Frenchmen to have served with the Germans during World War II), Costamanga, and André Bayle.

CHAPTER IX

Hell in the Snow: Pomerania

Seemingly a world away from the training grounds and recruits' barracks of Wildflecken, and the interminable factional squabbling of some of the Frenchmen, hundreds of miles away in the steadily falling snow of the Eastern Front the once all-conquering German military was dying.

A military machine that had stormed east on 22 June 1941, and had swept relentlessly forward to the very gates of Moscow, Leningrad and the Caucasus, was now being pushed just as relentlessly back from where they had come. The Wehrmacht now most resembled a punch drunk boxer, reeling constantly under blow after blow, but just too stubborn to fall down. By the end of November 1944 Germany had lost a truly staggering 5,914,844 men dead, missing and wounded on the Eastern Front, and the well of manpower was fast running dry. Her cities and factories, deluged by incendiary and blast bombs from the skies, were still operating, but could not hope to compete with the mass output of Soviet Russia and the USA, and even if they could Germany no longer had the men to man the machines. With the failure of the U-boats to starve Britain into submission, the Kriegsmarine had become largely superfluous to the war effort, and the once mighty Luftwaffe was lucky to be able to achieve even local air superiority in the East. And even then only for short periods over selected pieces of the Front; in the West even that modicum of effectiveness was a pipedream. Any hope Germany now had lay with the Army, and the Army needed men and it needed them now. The short life of Charlemagne would be entirely ruled by this reality.

Charlemagne gears for war

The Frenchmen of Charlemagne were always going to end up being deployed on the Russian Front, it was the *raison d'être* of their unit and their cause. The real question was always 'when and where', and those questions were being answered very quickly. Standard German practice had always been to place a new or refitted unit in a quiet sector to allow familiarisation and a certain 'breaking-in' period, when a unit could learn its craft and make its mistakes without facing the shock of major combat. A military unit is not a machine, but a collection of men and materiel that needs time and effort to create and nurture cohesion, and in combat it is cohesion that is the vital ingredient in effectiveness.

The premier units of the Waffen-SS relied utterly on that 'sense of self' which ensured that they continued to deliver impressive combat results despite the constant decimation and reformation they experienced. The structure of a division is a pyramid, with the foundations on which the unit is built being the individual rifle sections, then upwards to the platoons, the companies, the battalions, and finally up to the regiments that constitute the division's fighting components. While these units at all levels will have set operating procedures, this 'rule book', the unit standard operating procedures, is only half the story. Standard operating procedures are there to provide a uniform base for a unit, but are not intended to cover every eventuality. It is up to unit commanders at all levels to adapt, amend and introduce the way that suits the character of the unit they lead. This unwritten 'body of action' becomes the lifeblood of the unit and familiarity with it essential for combat effectiveness and survival.

To give a modern example, a newly-commissioned officer in a British Army infantry battalion might well take two hours or more to give his platoon a set of orders for a night fighting patrol, followed by probably an hour of practical rehearsals on the ground before the operation even starts. As the platoon adjusts to their new officer, and, more importantly, the platoon sergeant and section commanders teach him more of his trade, this significant amount of operational time will be steadily reduced down to less than an hour in total without damaging effectiveness or compromising the operation. Everybody gets to know everybody else and how they think and act. This saves enormous amounts of time and effort, and when perfected the unit is a magnificent fighting machine, working at a tempo that is truly awesome to behold on operations. This knowledge and operational familiarity pervades all levels of the military pyramid, and is just as necessary at battalion and regimental level in order to turn a formation into a fighting tool. It is one of those key characteristics of a military unit that is especially evident if it is missing, and when it is present everything 'just works'. The Germans, past masters of the art of warfare, were extremely aware of this need, and during the early years of the war it was standard practice for a rotational system to be in place at the Front to allow that vital shaking out time, but this was no longer possible on the Russian Front of 1945 when there was no such thing as a quiet sector or a quiet time.

Where's the fire?

Waffen-SS units were now accepted by all as the fire brigades of the Third Reich, being rushed to wherever the action was at its hottest, so this would see Charlemagne as a new SS formation, being lined up for one of the Eastern Front's many flashpoints. However, not being armoured or motorised would inevitably restrict their use and location, almost certainly to a more defensive role than the elite panzer and panzer grenadier Waffen-SS formations. Only the 1st Leibstandarte, 2nd Das Reich, 3rd Totenkopf, 5th Wiking, 9th Frundsberg, 10th Hohenstaufen and 12th Hitlerjugend SS Divisions were fully-fledged panzer divisions by 1945. Then in terms of combat utility came the panzer grenadier divisions, consisting of a combination of tanks and infantry. These were the 4th Polizei, 11th Nordland, 16th Reichsführer-SS, 17th Götz von Berlichingen and 18th Horst Wessel. In the main these panzer and panzer grenadier units spent the vast majority of their service time on the Russian Front (although the 17th Götz von Berlichingen was the exception being deployed only in the West), and where they were was always a good indicator of the German military's main point of effort.

The southern and central sections of the Eastern Front were still, in Hitler's mind, areas with potential for large-scale Nazi victories, while in the north on the Baltic the so-called 'battle of the European SS' on the Narva reflected Hitler's view of this sector as one of stubborn defence, and not best suited to his grandiose offensive fantasies. Thus the Soviet siege of Budapest was to be met by a German counter-offensive led by the tried and trusted 6th SS Panzer Army and its armoured spearheads, where a 'foot slogger's' unit such as Charlemagne would be of limited value. Far better, in the minds of German military planners, to commit the new unit to the northern sector where mobility was less of a necessity and where the much vaunted Waffen-SS defensive tenacity could play a key role. The foreign volunteers who made up the mass of Felix Steiner's 3rd Germanisches SS Panzer Corps, and who had fought so successfully at the Narva, did so with limited armoured support but seemingly limitless endurance and courage, and with this example fresh in OKW's minds the northern sector of the Eastern Front looked a likely candidate for Charlemagne's destination.

True to a limited extent this strategy may have been, but one look at the map of Europe of January 1945 would also show that as the Soviets pushed west the crisis point for the Nazis in terms of defending the fatherland would surely be in the north and not the south. It was here that Germany extended farthest east with its provinces of East and West Prussia, Silesia and Pomerania, and of course in the north lay Stalin's ultimate goal, the city of Berlin and Hitler himself. True, it was through the central and southern fronts that the states of eastern and central Europe lay, and Stalin was fixed on turning these countries into a new Soviet empire that would support communist Russia's emergence as a world power. They would also act as a buffer zone from future western military aggression; after all Stalin was determined that Barbarossa could never happen again. But in those sectors lay still large German and allied forces, and crucially the majority of Nazi Germany's remaining armoured units, who were also far away from Berlin.

Stalin's insistence on capturing Berlin was not of the level of obsession that Hitler disastrously fostered for Stalingrad back in 1942, but it cannot be underestimated. The Soviets deliberately misled the Western Allies as to their intentions for Berlin, playing on Eisenhower's fears, in particular of the non-existent Alpine Redoubt in the south of Germany, in order to have a clear run at conquering Berlin. Stalin would also be helped in achieving his aim by an increasingly unbalanced Nazi Führer. Hitler was obsessed with the illusions of impossible grand victories in the south of the Eastern Front, as Germany's last elite units and material were concentrated more and more to cover Hungary and Vienna, when the true nexus of events was far north on the Oder and Vistula rivers. Desperate to shore up the overstretched forces in the north of Germany, Charlemagne's future was ordained. Waffen-SS steadfast defence was called for and Charlemagne fitted the bill. What impact could such a small number of men have in a war that measured armies in the millions? This question would be answered in the snows of Pomerania and the rubble of Berlin.

Situation enemy forces: Pomerania

The end of 1944 had seen the Red Army push hard into eastern Europe and threaten both the Balkans and eastern Germany. Hitler and the OKW had managed, through careful husbandry, to put together one last offensive strike force, equipped with the best weaponry, most notably armour, that Nazi Germany could provide. That force could have presented the Red Army with a serious threat at the end of 1944 as it was operating at the end of often stretched supply lines, and with worn out men and equipment. It was not to be and instead, for strategic reasons, Germany's last Blitzkrieg army was hurled at the Americans in the thinly-held Ardennes in a race for the Meuse and Antwerp. Hitler gambled on dealing the Western Allies a crippling blow that would give him the time to turn east and throw the Soviets back onto the steppes. This was pure fantasy! The Ardennes was a hugely costly failure that saw irreplaceable men and equipment squandered in the snow.

Meanwhile back on the Eastern Front the Red Army was fast preparing for a new offensive. Just as with Operation Bagration the previous summer, this would be a massive assault across a wide front, carried out by overwhelmingly strong forces. Its aim was the destruction of Nazi Germany, and if possible, the capture of Berlin and the ending of the war. In the northern sector the immediate goal was to drive for the Baltic coast and cut East Prussia off from the rest of Germany. As this was being achieved the Russians would also push west, reach and cross the Oder river, and then a decision would be taken on the viability of pushing on to take Berlin or halting to regroup.

To accomplish this set of objectives the Red Army mustered Zhukov's 1st and Rokossovsky's 2nd White Russian Fronts, truly powerful forces with an overwhelming superiority in men and material over the German forces they faced grouped in the much weakened 2nd and 9th Armies.

On 12 January 1945 the Russians launched their offensive from the Baranow bridgehead, closely followed on the 14th by Rokossovsky's attack on the 2nd Army Front. Fighting was heavy and casualties high on both sides. The Soviet assault divisions came up against prepared German positions and the ferocious counter-attacks of the elite Grossdeutschland Panzer Corps; these combined to bleed the first echelon Russian units white. However the sheer weight of the offensive was too much for the depleted German formations to hold, and by the 18th the Front had been breached and the Russians were driving west and north-west.

The East Prussian border was crossed by 20 January 1945, and the Red Army now stood on German soil. The town of Tannenberg, a powerful and historic symbol of German victory over Russia from the First World War and before, was taken on the 22nd, and on 26 January the Russians reached the Baltic coast north-east of Elbing. A large part of Germany was now cut-off, as were the forces of the 4th Army and the 3rd Panzer Army. Not yet finished the Soviets drove west and reached the banks of the fast flowing Oder river at the end of January. Berlin was now only forty miles away and barely defended.

A hasty German counter-offensive from Pomerania, launched by the foreign volunteers of the 11th SS Panzer-Grenadier-Freiwilligen-Division Nordland and the 23rd SS Panzer-Grenadier-Freiwilligen-Division Nederland did at least manage to throw the Soviets off balance and make them reconsider a thrust to Berlin. In the event STAVKA played safe and decided to wait before attacking the German capital. Of note here is that Reichsführer-SS Heinrich Himmler finally fulfilled his desire to command an army, when he was appointed to lead the newly-established Army Group Vistula. Himmler then proceeded very quickly to demonstrate that whilst he was a past master at running a continental European terror and slaughter machine, he was a truly appalling leader of men in battle, and was soon replaced.

Charlemagne to the east

Charlemagne was officially informed of its move to Pomerania on 15 February 1945. Just two days later, on the 17th the first convoy left

Wildflecken for the Eastern Front. The whole move would take over a fortnight, whereupon the Division would be concentrated and complete work-up training for another week before being committed to combat. This then was the plan. The Division was formed into its component parts and readied for deployment. Critical to an understanding of what transpired in Pomerania later on is a knowledge of German military practice for formations coming up to the line.

The German military system was built to encourage flexibility and allow the rapid movement of forces to whatever part of the Front they were most needed, either to reinforce success or cover enemy break-throughs. This rapid movement was possible for the men of the formations, but not for the huge amounts of heavy equipment these units used. The logistics alone in transporting a division's worth of support weapons was staggering, and so the German method of operation was to mass equipment in depots near the front line, independent of the units who would use it. A formation would then move to the Front, and behind the German lines would marry up with its equipment prior to going into battle. This *modus operandi* was used throughout the war by the Wehrmacht and proved incredibly resilient; however in Charlemagne's case it was to go disastrously wrong. Though still forming, the Division was to move to the Front with hardly any heavy equipment, and any inability to get hold of this kit prior to battle would see the French SS men come up against the armoured mass of the Red Army with little more than personal weapons.

Make-up and faces
The Division that headed east in mid-February had evolved very quickly from the hotch potch of men and units that had filled the barrack rooms in first Greifenberg and later Wildflecken.

Command of the Division was still in Edgar Puaud's hands but he had a German shadow as 'Inspector'. This general officer would not necessarily lead the Division, but he would provide the French commander with 'technical' advice. This was potentially an extremely difficult role to fulfil as it could easily be seen as an imposition; to carry out the role well would require an individual with special skills. The man selected for this tricky work was one SS-Brigadeführer Dr Gustav Krukenberg. Krukenberg was a 56-year-old ex-lawyer from Bonn who had served with distinction during World War I, then worked in numerous positions in both the private and public sectors between the wars, including butting heads with Joseph Goebbels at the Propaganda Ministry. Going back to active service at the beginning of World War II, he served on both the Western and Eastern Fronts, lately as Chief-of-Staff for the Waffen-SS 6th Corps and then the famous 3rd Germanisches SS Panzer Corps in the Baltic states. He was a good choice for his role with the Charlemagne, a fluent French speaker and experienced in the raising and training of foreign SS volunteers. However, he was no Panzer Meyer or Jochen Peiper, and would provide steady if uninspired leadership. This indeed was a general accusation levelled at the Waffen-SS on innumerable occasions, that while its private soldiers were all potential NCOs, and all its NCOs potential company officers, its officers were only accomplished at up to regimental level. Anything above that was beyond the vast majority of them, with officers such as Fritz Witt, Peiper and Meyer being true exceptions. After all the high level commanders, Paul Hausser and Felix Steiner, were both ex-Army and not 'pure' Waffen-SS. So in true Waffen-SS style Krukenberg would be competent, but nothing more.

What of the other key Divisional appointments, who would lead the Charlemagne into battle? Now the Miliciens had arrived there was a certain amount of reshuffling and internal politicking. As well as achieving combat effectiveness there was a need to balance the major component parts of the formation to ensure the LVF, the SS-Sturmbrigade Frankreich and the Milice were all represented and felt that their voices were heard in the Division's affairs. As commander Puaud was ex-LVF, and he took the excellent ex-Milicien *chef* from Paris, Jean de Vaugelas, as his Chief-of-Staff. Vaugelas was a leading light of the Milice, and had fought well against the Maquis in the Haute-Savoie operations of 1943.

To lead Waffen-Grenadier Regiment der SS 57, based on a hard core of ex-SS-Sturmbrigade Frankreich men, the Germans initially appointed the SS-Sturmbrigade's old commander, Gamory-Dubourdeau. This was merely a holding appointment, and the Breton soon moved on to the SS Main Office in Berlin and was replaced by the newly-promoted Waffen-Sturmbannführer Pierre Cance of Galician fame. However, although ex-SS-Sturmbrigade he was considered far too close politically to Darnard, and was swiftly removed in favour of another ex-Milicien, Waffen-Hauptsturmführer Victor de Bourmont. De Bourmont was a minor French nobleman, a short and precise man who believed in leading from the front and sharing hardships with his men. He was a career soldier, after graduating from Saint-Cyr he served abroad in the Empire in a Tunisian Tirailleur regiment, before returning home and fighting the Germans in 1940. He subsequently joined the Milice and was promoted to the rank of Capitaine serving under the command of de Vaugelas. His Regiment was organised and commanded as follows:

- Waffen-Grenadier Regiment der SS 57
- Main Regimental units:
  Infantry Gun Company (9/57) : Waffen-Hauptsturmführer Robert
  Roy (ex-NSKK and SS-Sturmbrigade)

Anti-tank Company (10/57)   : Waffen-Obersturmführer Labuze
        (ex-Milice)

Recce Platoon   : Waffen-Untersturmführer Erdozain

Engineers Platoon   : Waffen-Standartenoberjunker Jean-Pierre
        Lefevre (ex-SS-Sturmbrigade)

Signals Platoon   : Waffen-Untersturmführer Brucard (pseudonym)

- 1st Battalion (1/57)   : Waffen-Obersturmführer Henri Fenet
        (ex-SS-Sturmbrigade)

1st Company   : Waffen-Untersturmführer Brazier

2nd Company   : Waffen-Obersturmführer Yvan Bartolomei
        (ex-SS-Sturmbrigade)

3rd Company   : Waffen-Untersturmführer Counil
        (ex-SS-Sturmbrigade)

4th Company   : Waffen-Oberscharführer Couvreur
        (ex-SS-Sturmbrigade)

- 2nd Battalion (2/57)   : Waffen-Hauptsturmführer René-Andre Obitz
        (ex-LVF)

5th Company   : Waffen-Oberscharführer Lucien Hennecart
        (ex-SS-Sturmbrigade)

6th Company   : Waffen-Untersturmführer Albert

7th Company   : Waffen-Standartenoberjunker Million-
        Rousseau

8th Company   : Waffen-Untersturmführer Philippe Colnion
        (ex-SS-Sturmbrigade)

Waffen-Grenadier Regiment der SS 58 was based on old LVF men, and as such had probably the most combat experience in the Division, but that was tempered by a certain laxity in discipline which permeated these ex-legionnaires, and explained the often poor physical and mental state of some of the men after almost three years of warfare and extreme conditions on the Russian Front. To lead the Regiment the Germans appointed another ex-Milicien, Emile Raybaud. Raybaud was a colleague and friend of both de Bourmont and de Vaugelas having served with both before and during the war. Like de Bourmont, Raybaud was a professional soldier who had served in the elite Chasseurs Alpins after graduating from Saint-Cyr. He too had fought the Germans in 1940, before joining the Milice. He was a larger than life character, tall and powerful with no time for political in-fighting. However, he was an ardent French nationalist and anti-communist, and as such was a natural choice to lead the ex-LVF men in Regiment 58. That unit's order of battle was as follows:

- Waffen-Grenadier Regiment der SS 58
- Main Regimental units:
  Infantry Gun Company (9/58) : Waffen-Obersturmführer Français
  (ex-SS- Sturmbrigade)
  Anti-tank Company (10/58) : Waffen-Oberscharführer Girard
  (ex-LVF)
  Recce Platoon & Signals : Waffen-Hauptscharführer Gobion (ex-LVF)
  Engineers Platoon : Unknown
- 1st Battalion (1/58) : Waffen-Hauptsturmführer Emile Monneuse
  (ex-Milice)

  1st Company : Waffen-Obersturmführer Fatin (ex-LVF)
  2nd Company : Waffen-Obersturmführer Géromini
  3rd Company : Waffen-Untersturmführer Yves Rigeade
  (ex-LVF)
  4th Company : Waffen-Obersturmführer André Tardan
  (ex-Milice)

- 2nd Battalion (2/58) : Waffen-Hauptsturmführer Maurice Berret
  (ex-LVF)
  5th Company : Waffen-Obersturmführer Georges Wagner
  (ex-LVF)
  6th Company : Waffen-Obersturmführer Michel Saint-Magne
  (ex-LVF)
  7th Company : Waffen-Hauptscharführer Eric Walter (ex-LVF)
  8th Company : Waffen-Obersturmführer Paul Defever
  (ex-LVF)

The Divisional units of note were the following:

Compagnie d'Honneur: SS-Obersturmführer Wilhelm Weber
(ex-SS Germania)
Panzerjäger Battalion : Waffen-Sturmbannführer Jean Boudet-Gheusi
(ex-LVF)
Anti-aircraft Company : Waffen-Untersturmführer René Fayard
(ex-SS-Sturmbrigade)
Anti-tank Company : Waffen-Obersturmführer Serge Krotoff
(ex-SS-Sturmbrigade)
Assault Gun Company : Waffen-Obersturmführer Pierre Michel
(ex-LVF and SS-Sturmbrigade)
Artillery Group : Waffen-Hauptsturmführer Jean Havette

These then were the men and their commands. Levels of experience and competence varied widely, but of real concern to both Puaud and Krukenberg was that there were very few officers, even before battle was joined. A relatively small number of casualties among key personnel would effectively render the Division headless. Both Bobr and the Galician battles had amply demonstrated the huge attrition of leaders in battle, particularly at platoon and company level. This was both as a result of the Waffen-SS style of leadership, but also a hallmark of fighting on the Eastern Front. Russian snipers liked nothing more than a German officer in their sights. To maintain effectiveness there has to be sufficient command and control, and it was obvious that even a short battle would cause significant loss of commanders and therefore greatly reduce the formations combat effectiveness.

To the Front!

The different convoys of Frenchmen began to arrive in the Divisional concentration area towards the end of February. However, whilst in transit the situation at the Front had altered dramatically. On 22 February the Soviets launched an offensive with the 19th Army and the 3rd Guards Tank Corps, part of the 2nd White Russian Front. The aim of the offensive was to reach the Baltic through Neustettin and Körlin. This would split Pomerania in two, and would crush any hope the Germans might have of punching south from the coast and cutting off the Russian spearheads heading towards Berlin. In short it was an exercise in flank protection, but one carried out by the now customarily huge Soviet forces and firepower, the Soviets mustering six infantry, three mechanised and three tank divisions, plus a number of artillery and rocket divisions. The German forces opposing them were only the two depleted divisions of General Hochbaum's 18th Gebirgs (Mountain) Corps, part of 2nd Army, which itself was part of Army Group Vistula.

Charlemagne was to come under command of the weakened 18th Gebirgs Corps. The Corps consisted of the 32nd Infantry Division and the 15th Waffen-Grenadier Division der SS (lettische Nr.1). These were two excellent formations. The 32nd was a Pomeranian unit, and the men were determined to do all they could to protect their homes and families, while the SS division was one of the three first class Baltic units; its Latvian volunteers had already lost their homeland to the Russian advance but were making the Soviets pay for every inch of ground. The problem was not the quality of the Corps, this was excellent, it was rather their numbers. Both units had been in constant action for over a month already and had suffered terrible casualties, and were still meant to hold a sector of Front some forty-five kilometres long. It was hoped by Army Group that the

Charlemagne would be able to take responsibility for a significant length of the line to allow the creation of local reserves, but the Frenchmen weren't there yet, and the Soviets acted first.

Dawn on the 24th saw five fresh Soviet divisions slam into the weakened and overstretched 32nd Division. Within hours the front line was ripped apart and the Russians streamed north. For the forward elements of Charlemagne located in Hammerstein, that meant the Red Army was less than twenty kilometres away, and still there was no sign of their heavy equipment. Even though much of the Division was still in transit, Puaud and Krukenberg had no option but to deploy the troops they did have to meet the Soviets hurtling towards them. The troops were positioned east and south of Hammerstein, with I/57 under Fenet defending Heinrichswalde, and II/57 under Obitz north-east in Barkenfelde. Monneuse's I/58 was placed at Bärenwalde to the north, so that the formation was forming a hard shoulder running south–north to deflect the Red Army advance.

The Russian wave hits

The three French battalions were now facing massed Soviet assaults with no heavy weapons in support. The fighting was severe with Obitz's II/57 in particular coming under huge pressure. However, in the nick of time Krotoff brought up his twelve anti-tank guns and the Soviet attacks were stopped dead.

Fenet's battalion fared even worse, as on arriving at Heinrichswalde they found it had already been occupied in strength by the Russians. Fenet launched a full battalion attack on the night on the 24th, when a lack of ammunition for the battalion's mortars meant the assaulting companies had to take the village at bayonet point. The fighting was bloody, with both sides taking, then losing, then retaking, house after house in the burning ruins of the small Pomeranian village. Bartolomei's Company in particular was hit hard and suffered severe casualties including losing two platoon commanders killed. The outcome of the attack was still in the balance when strong Red Army forces began to flood around Fenet's flanks threatening to encircle and destroy his command. The battalion withdrew, but in the confusion, and with no radios for communication, it splintered. Bartolomei's Company received direct verbal orders from de Bourmont to head back towards Hammerstein, whilst Fenet was moving his other companies to Bärenwalde.

Back in Bärenwalde itself the II/57 wiped out another attacking Soviet force of company strength during the night of the 24th, but was then swamped at daybreak by an entire Siberian division! Obitz tried desperately to extricate his men to the railway line to the north, but the Siberians

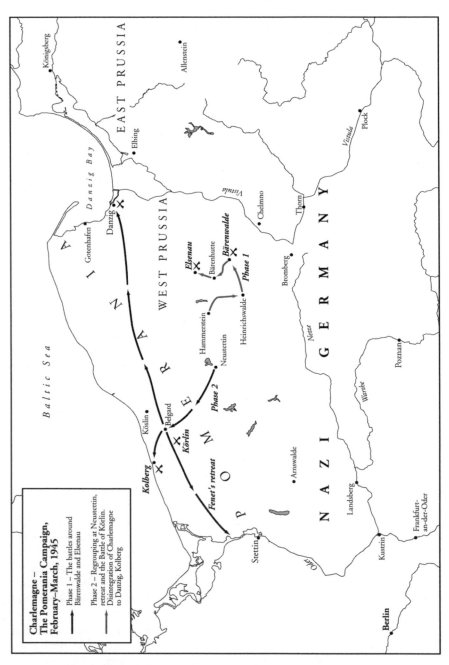

Charlemagne – The Pomeranian Campaign, February–March 1945

were in among his positions and the grenadiers took fearful casualties. Not only was the battalion badly beaten up, but its pell-mell retreat left both Regimental Headquarters and Monneuse's neighbouring I/58 exposed to Soviet flanking attack. De Bourmont managed to withdraw his Headquarters before being hit, but Monneuse was not so lucky. Having deployed his battalion, and trying in vain to contact his flanking units to establish a solid defensive line, he soon found himself under heavy Soviet attack. The battle began to degenerate into a series of vicious dogfights between individual French platoons and companies and much larger numbers of Russians. As the I/58 tried desperately to fend off the Soviet frontal attacks, other Red Army units swept round the sides of the battling Frenchmen, and very soon they were surrounded. Despite the desperate situation his unit was in, Monneuse didn't panic and calmly ordered a break-out with Géromini's Company leading. Géromini himself, a fiery Corsican, charged out front with his men and hit the astonished Russians hard. Punching through their lines he led the battalion back east through the woods towards the Hammerstein–Bärenwalde railway line. Contact was briefly made with Fenet's battalion during the retreat, but it was soon obvious that overall command of the fighting had broken down, and it was now down to the battalion commanders to get their men out of this. By now the 32nd Pomeranian Division had been totally brushed aside and the full force of the Soviet offensive was being brought to bear on the sector of Front manned by Charlemagne. There were now no fewer than twelve Soviet divisions, including three tank divisions, lining up to smash their way through the massively outnumbered and outgunned French Waffen-SS men. If they were not significantly reinforced or heavily supported by strong anti-tank and artillery elements, then disaster loomed.

Battle on the railway line

By midday on the 25th Fenet and his I/57 were completely detached from the rest of the Division, and he ended up withdrawing on his own initiative back to Hammerstein. Here he expected to meet up with other Divisional elements, but the camp was deserted. However, he had some good fortune when 2nd Company marched into the camp with the wily old campaigner Ivan Bartolomei at its head. The battalion was now reunited.

Back on the Hammerstein–Bärenwalde railway line the II/57 and the I/58 were busily being formed into some sort of hasty defensive line by Krukenberg and Puaud, both of whom were also trying to deploy other Divisional units as they appeared. Crucially this included Roy's, Girard's and even Krotoff's anti-tank companies, as well as every mortar that the Frenchmen could lay their hands on, and the Divisional combat engineer company. For the first time in the battle the Frenchmen had been able to concentrate a reasonable amount of firepower, and it was these heavy units that would be vital in trying to stave off the advancing Soviets with their preponderance of tanks. Divisional Headquarters was established in the nearby village of Elsenau, and here Krukenberg took control of the Division. It had become obvious very quickly that Puaud was out of his depth trying to fight a divisional battle. A fine leader of men and personally brave, he had neither the temperament, training nor experience to coordinate the diverse and complex elements that were involved in fighting a division. He remained at Divisional Headquarters but Krukenberg gave the orders, and one of his first was to relieve Waffen-Hauptsturmführer René-André Obitz of command of the II/57 for incompetence.

The Frenchmen were now deployed on the railway line, with a key position being a level crossing that cut right through the railway embankment. Behind them were more woods, and there were also a few scattered farmhouses and outbuildings in the area. Their fields of fire to the front were broken up by more trees, but they did have cover to their rear, either back to Hammerstein to the west or north to Elsenau, in the event of a retreat. Their real weaknesses were in ammunition and manpower. The two grenadier battalions had been severely mauled by the earlier Soviet attacks around Bärenwalde, and they were now thin on the ground. That laid even more importance on the heavy weapons companies, but both the anti-tank and infantry howitzers had only light scales of ammunition. The lack of available transport had restricted how much ammo could be taken forward and there was little hope of any more being brought up.

Scratchy positions were in place by midday just as the Red Army began a series of violent assaults on the thinly held French positions. The Russians coordinated their attacks with armour and overwhelming artillery fire and the Frenchmen were constantly having to shift position to keep out of the eye of the storm and keep fighting. Albert's Company was lucky, in particular, by somehow avoiding annihilation as it moved exposed out in the open along the railway line to a better position. Waves of screaming Soviet infantry swept onto the French guns and were mercilessly cut down. Lines of T-34s charged forward only to be shot to pieces by Krotoff's guns in particular, and also by daring grenadiers who were using panzerfäusts abandoned by other German units. The fighting was confused and often hand to hand. In the mounting chaos Puaud finally came into his own, abandoning the Divisional Headquarters to Krukenberg, and taking de Vaugelas with him, he went from position to position along the line, encouraging his men and somehow escaping injury as bullets and shrapnel swept the field. Many a young grenadier would look up from his shallow trench to see Puaud kneeling behind him, machine gun round his neck, shouting him on to ever more resistance before he would run to the next hole in the ground. Somehow it worked, and for a few desperate hours the massive Red Army onslaught was held.

Russian casualties were dreadful. Whole companies were machine-gunned or blasted to oblivion by mortars and howitzers, and it was little better for the tank crews. Tank after tank was either set on fire, with the crewmen burning to death in the fiery coffin or being gunned down as they tried to escape, or obliterated by a direct hit that set off all the tank's ammunition. After those explosions there was little left of the tank or its crew. As long as the Charlemagne could keep up the withering fire on both the Soviet infantry and tanks then they could just hold. But ammo was running out fast. Then in a matter of minutes the battle turned as Krotoff's guns were caught in the open by a huge artillery barrage and the company was almost wiped out. As Krotoff's guns fell silent the Russians seized their chance and surged forward towards the level crossing in an attempt to finally break the stubborn French line. Finally overwhelming numbers paid off and the victorious Russians seized the level crossing and shattered the Charlemagne's position. The line disintegrated as commanders tried desperately to get their men away from the charging Russians. Roy fired off the last rounds for his remaining guns, spiked those that couldn't be moved and retreated fast towards the small village of Bärenhutte.

The field now belonged to the Russians. In a relatively small piece of land there were wrecked tank hulks and bodies everywhere. The French dead were clustered around their positions where they had fought off the increasingly heavy attacks, and in front of their gun barrels lay hundreds of Soviet dead in their earth brown smocks.

The splintering begins

Charlemagne was now beginning to be torn apart, and its ability to fight as a Division was under serious threat. Back at Hammerstein was Fenet and the I/57, while at Elsenau, having retreated from the railway line battle, was de Bourmont and the remnants of II/57, along with Fatin's and Géromini's companies from I/58. The remainder of I/58 was with Monneuse retreating to Bärenhutte. There were also isolated groups of stragglers all over the battlefield.

Waiting at Bärenhutte was Emile Raybaud, temporarily having no command as his 1st Battalion was deployed under his friend de Bourmont, until Berret's II/58 arrived on the morning of the 25th just as the desperate battle for the railway line was getting underway. Raybaud decided to hold the battalion in Bärenhutte, apart from Saint-Magne's company which was sent out on defence duties, until he had a clear picture of the situation. Now Monneuse was streaming back into Bärenhutte with the best part of two companies, along with Roy's men and a few light guns.

It was obvious to Raybaud that the Division was in serious trouble. Much of the Division's already severely limited heavy equipment had been lost at the railway line, as well as the large numbers of grenadiers lying dead in the snow. He reacted by getting a grip of the troops and reorganising them into a viable defensive ring based on Bärenhutte. Luckily for the Frenchmen the Russians saw Bärenhutte as a backwater and their columns bypassed it, and so the SS men got a much-needed breathing space, but the village was now cut off from the rest of Charlemagne.

Elsenau was not as lucky as Bärenhutte. It was on the main Soviet axis of advance and was now directly in the path of the Russian steamroller. Krukenberg warned his Corps Commander, General Hochbaum, that he would be unable to defend Elsenau, but Hochbaum was desperate that the Russians be stopped to allow the rest of the Corps to fall back and re-establish a new defence line around the town of Stegers, and so Krukenberg was ordered to hold at all costs. The stage was now set for a true David and Goliath contest at Elsenau. Krukenberg had a mixed bag of companies from both Regiments der SS 57 and 58, but they had no heavy weapons. All in all there were only some 400 French SS grenadiers in Elsenau who were still capable of fighting. However Krukenberg also had Weber's as yet untested Compagnie d'Honneur. This unit was only some eighty strong, but they had two distinct advantages. Firstly they were armed with armfuls of panzerfäusts from a depot in Hammerstein, and secondly they had undergone the training of Wilhelm Weber. This young German officer was an incredibly tough ex-SS Germania man, who had learnt his trade as a small unit commander in the harshest fights on the Russian Front. Weber had utilised all his experience in preparing and training his men. All of the Charlemagne men underwent the standard, rigorous Waffen-SS training regimen but for Weber and the Compagnie d'Honneur that was only the start point. At the end of a hard day's training when the infantry companies stood down for the evening, it was Weber's men who would carry on, stretching already tired muscles with punishing night marches and weapons drill. At first the rest of Charlemagne had laughed at the ever-tired volunteers in the Compagnie d'Honneur, but soon enough they were recognised for the elite they were becoming. Grenadiers began to view the volunteers with envy as they saw them build a recognisable *esprit de corps* that marked them out from their fellow Frenchmen. They were most definitely the Charlemagne elite, and now they were going to prove it.

T-34s against Weber's men

Krukenberg threw the Compagnie d'Honneur out to the front of Elsenau to provide advance warning of the Red Army vanguards and to try to slow their advance up, whilst he tried to organise the rest of his men.

So the Russian strike force of close on a dozen divisions, that had just a few hours before broken two entire Charlemagne battalions supported by all the Division's heavy weapons, were now racing forward straight into a force of just eighty men armed with nothing more than personal weapons and hand held anti-tank weapons with a range of less than 100 metres. To camouflage themselves against the snow Weber's men took sheets from a local farm and tore them up as makeshift coveralls, then dug hasty trenches covering the road from Elsenau to Bärenwalde. There were woods scattered around the position, with large pieces of open ground, but where the road and tracks ran through trees there was good cover for ambushes.

The Compagnie didn't have long to wait before a column of T-34s appeared and began to advance towards Elsenau. The tracks of the T-34s crunched over the crisp snow as they rolled confidently forward. The only other sound was the far-off background noise of artillery, but the Russians were in relaxed mood, not expecting any resistance to their advance. In their hastily dug slit trenches the freezing SS grenadiers had to just lie and wait as the noise from the approaching Soviets grew and grew. Clutching panzerfäusts and machine guns they strained to hear the order that would see them confront their enemy for the first time. Waiting until the last possible moment, Weber shouted the order to 'Fire!', and the grenadiers rose from their holes and fired their panzerfäusts point blank into the Soviet tanks. It was carnage. Machine guns stuttered as the Frenchmen raked the Soviet infantry accompanying the tanks, and panzerfäust after panzerfäust was poured into the mass of tanks. The French grenadiers ran from position to position firing at any tank they could see and that wasn't quick enough in trying to escape the slaughter. The ex-Kriegsmarine men in particular distinguished themselves with François Appolot and Eugène Vaulot, whom we will meet again in Berlin, destroying two tanks each. Weber led from the front as ever and knocked out three himself, and his example was followed by his entire unit who tore into the Soviet armour with glee, brewing up steel monster after steel monster.

Too late the Russian supporting infantry arrived on the scene in force, charging towards the handful of Frenchmen determined to get their revenge on the impudent SS men. But the Compagnie had been drilled too well, and calmly the grenadiers manned their machine guns and cut into the running mass of men. The charging Soviets fell in heaps, their lines raked by gunfire that tore huge holes in their ranks and sent them reeling back, leaving piles of dead comrades everywhere. Out of range, they were mustered by their officers and commissars and charged again, only to be met by the same withering hail of fire that bowled men off their feet in their dozens. Sent scurrying back the Soviets tried one last time to overwhelm the stubborn defenders, only to be butchered again by accurate and heavy fire laid down by the cool and determined Frenchmen. Shocked and dazed the Soviets held back, preferring to bring down heavy artillery and tank fire on the exposed positions and bypass them on the flanks. Weber knew the game was up. He had already lost a lot of his brave grenadiers and those who were left were in danger of being pulverised by the weight of Russian fire. He took the only sensible decision and withdrew his remaining men in good order around 1730hrs. They had held the Soviet advance for a good three hours and in front of their positions were nineteen burning Russian tanks and several hundred dead Red Army soldiers. It was a dramatic victory and one that would give heart to the rest of Elsenau's defenders.

Last stand in the cemetery
The fight for Elsenau now became a fight for the cemetery which dominated the whole village. To hold it was to hold Elsenau, and so the remains of three companies from both Regiments der SS 57 and 58 were positioned to defend it against the advancing Soviets. The battle mirrored the earlier fight of the Compagnie d'Honneur, with the outnumbered French grenadiers, armed with nothing more than personal weapons and panzerfäusts, struggling to hold attack after attack by massed tanks and infantry. Smoke from burning tanks and buildings shrouded the battle so that all was confusion and the fighting came down to hand to hand with bayonet and entrenching tool, as French SS men stabbed and gouged their Red Army opponents to death among the gravestones. Tanks would appear out of the smoke belching fire from their main armament and machine guns, only to be blown to pieces by panzerfäusts fired at distances of a few metres. The battle see-sawed back and forth with gains measured in yards, until the Russians threw in one last supreme effort and, on their fifth attempt, threw the surviving Charlemagne men out of the cemetery. With the loss of the cemetery Elsenau couldn't be held and the surviving defenders streamed away in an effort to escape the Russian torrent. They left many of their number behind in the burning ruins of Elsenau. In particular Weber's Compagnie d'Honneur had paid a high price for its defiance, losing half their number.

Raybaud and Bärenhutte
Back at Bärenhutte, Raybaud busied his men by having them fire continuously at the Russian convoys heading past on the road to Elsenau, but soon enough they were running out of ammunition and under direct attack. Under cover of darkness Bärenhutte was abandoned and Raybaud led his men back to Hammerstein on the morning of 26 February. In Hammerstein all was chaos, and as it couldn't be held a further retreat

was ordered back to Neustettin. Units, part units, groups and stragglers from Charlemagne all streamed away from Hammerstein and the victorious Red Army, towards the temporary security of Neustettin. By midday on the 26th most survivors of the earlier fighting had reached the town, but were in desperate need of reorganisation. Many had been in constant combat for the last forty-eight hours. They had eaten little and slept even less. The majority had lost most of their equipment, including a number who had even lost their weapons, and they were shocked and dazed after being in the eye of the Soviet storm for the last two days. Casualties were huge. As the unit was splintered it was difficult to get an accurate picture, but at least 1,000 men had been killed, with another 1,000 wounded or missing. But Pomerania was not yet finished with Charlemagne; there would be more brutal fighting to come.

Retreat: Neustettin to Belgard

Puaud was in Neustettin having escaped from Elsenau, but Krukenberg was still fighting his way through the Soviets. So, having assessed the situation with his officers, Puaud knew the decision was clear: the town could not be held and the Frenchmen must carry on retreating. Orders were given for a withdrawal of some eighty kilometres north to Belgard starting at dawn the next morning, the 27th. It was not a moment too soon. As the Frenchmen were preparing to leave the Russians flooded into the town shooting up everything they could find. As a result Puaud was forced to deploy a scratch force of some 250 men to try to delay the Russian follow-up so as to allow the remainder of the Division to disengage and put some distance between themselves and the pursuing Red Army. Alongside an equally scratch force of Wehrmacht men, the French rearguard stood and fought for Neustettin throughout the entire day, being hit by concentrated artillery and tank attacks supported by air strikes from the Red airforce. The fighting was soon house-to-house, but by late afternoon the job was done and the defenders could disengage and retreat. This was completed in some disorder, but at last the Charlemagne abandoned Neustettin to its fate and headed north after their comrades to Belgard. They left another hundred or so of their comrades behind in the town as the Frenchmen continued to pay in blood for their defiance in Pomerania.

Belgard and reorganisation

The march to Belgard was a nightmare of cold, hunger and sore feet. The wind swept in from the Baltic and through the shredded uniforms of the exhausted grenadiers. Food was scarce and there was no chance to stop and light fires. Instead the SS men kept trudging along, encouraged by

Puaud who was inexhaustible as he cheered his men on. Incredibly the Frenchmen covered the eighty kilometres from Neustettin to their rally point in the city in twenty-four hours, but on arrival they were sorely in need of a rest and refit. They were to get neither. Krukenberg was waiting for them, having escaped from Elsenau, and he immediately set about reorganising the Division for further combat.

A Régiment de Marche (RM) of two battalions was formed made up of the best of the survivors, those most willing and able to carry on fighting, while the remainder were formed into a Régiment de Reserve (RR). Command of the Régiment de Marche went to Emile Raybaud, and he had Fenet and Jean Bassompierre as his two battalion commanders. Their battalions of four companies each were constituted on the same basis as Regiments der SS 57 and 58, in that Fenet's I/RM was predominantly ex-SS-Sturmbrigade, and Bassompierre's II/RM was mostly ex-LVF.

Victor de Bourmont was given command of the Régiment de Reserve, and his structure was the same as Raybaud's, with Monneuse and Berret leading I/RR and II/RR respectively. Again, as in the Régiment de Marche, much of Monneuse's I/RR battalion was ex-SS-Sturmbrigade and Berret's II/RR was ex-LVF.

The Company commanders of the two restructured regiments were generally of high quality with men such as Walter, Rigeade, Hennecart and Couvreur taking up posts. All commanders then went about their business getting their commands into some kind of shape for the action to come. This preparation took up all of 1 March 1945. On 2 March the Division was ordered to move to the town of Körlin and defend it, in order to protect the Corps' retreat to the coastal city of Kolberg. If the Red Army could take Körlin then they could threaten the entire retreat and annihilate the German forces. Charlemagne was being called to a desperate battle once again.

Körlin

Only some eight kilometres from Belgard, Körlin was a town of strategic significance as it was the hub of the main highways to Kolberg and Stettin. Control of the town gave the occupier control of the road network. It was a strong defensive position being surrounded on three sides by the Persante river and a tributary, with access to the town via several bridges. That made it easier to defend, and that at least favoured the Charlemagne. Raybaud set up his Headquarters in the main square with Fenet's I/RM in the south-east of the town covering the Belgard road, and Bassompierre's II/RM in the north-east covering the Körlin road.

The grenadiers wasted no time digging in and preparing their positions for the inevitable Red Army assault. De Bourmont's command drew the short straw and had to cover a series of possible crossing points over the Persante river. This meant the under-strength and pretty demoralised Régiment de Reserve had a Front to defend of over twenty-two kilometres; this was impossible for a non-mechanised unit. The French concentrated all their remaining support weapons to defend the town. They also grabbed any weapons they could from passing German stragglers on the roads, but they were still desperately short of the necessities of successful defence, including anti-tank and infantry guns, artillery support and engineering defence stores such as mines and wire.

However, it wasn't all bad news for Charlemagne. As Raybaud's men were digging in they were astonished to see a column of fresh troops march into town. Not only were these men fresh, they were French! A battalion of reinforcements from Greifenberg had been assembled and sent up to the Front, and here they were. The battalion was some 500 men strong and commanded by Waffen-Hauptsturmführer Michel Bisiau, a 30-year-old ex-LVF man. He had three strong companies led by Waffen-Untersturmführer Paul Pignard-Berthet, ex-SS-Sturmbrigade, Waffen-Hauptsturmführer Georges Flamand, ex-LVF, and lastly Waffen-Obersturmführer Cyrille de Bregeot, ex-SS-Sturmbrigade. These were the first reinforcements the Charlemagne had ever received and they were welcomed with open arms by their comrades. The arrival of Bisiau's men meant that by the end of 3 March the strength of Charlemagne stood at a reasonable 4,000. But the fortunes of war were not with the French, and as they prepared their defences in Körlin Soviet thrusts swept around the town to the north and south. Strong Soviet tank units first took the village of Gross Jestin to the west of Körlin, and then spurred on to reach the suburbs of Kolberg early on the morning of 4 March. Charlemagne was now encircled and behind the Red Army front lines!

Lost cause

The dawning of 4 March also brought the first Soviet probes towards Körlin. Initially the Soviet fire was not heavy, but around midday a strong force of tanks and infantry put in a concerted attack on the town, only to be repulsed by French fire. But as ever the Russians were not easily put off, and the ferocity of the assaults grew steadily throughout the afternoon. Hordes of Soviet infantry streamed forward, trying to rush the bridges and ford the Persante to establish a bridgehead. Their casualties were awesome. The French machine gun barrels glowed red hot as belt after belt of ammunition was poured into the Russians, but nothing seemed to stop them. More and more Soviet infantrymen kept on coming, seemingly oblivious to their dead comrades strewn across the battlefield. But little by little their numbers and courage paid off and the SS grenadiers were pushed back. Suddenly they were across the river and had a bridgehead. If they could reinforce it quickly enough it would be the beginning of the end for the defence of Körlin. But the French weren't finished yet. It was Fenet who reacted first and fastest. He scraped together every man who could hold a gun and led them in a desperate counter-attack to throw back the Russians. The fight was short and vicious. Many of the attacking French grenadiers were already wounded, but they all knew that if the Russians weren't thrown back then Körlin was finished. The bridgehead was wiped out and the defenders had bought themselves a breathing space. But the noose round them was getting tighter.

Get west!

By evening the situation had become untenable. Körlin was completely cut off, and to avoid death or capture it was obvious to all that the French had to abandon the town and break out. Krukenberg and Puaud put a plan together and briefed their officers. The plan was simple: using the cover of darkness the Division was to form up with Fenet's battalion leading, de Bourmont's Régiment de Reserve next and a rearguard of Bassompierre's battalion. The key was to travel light with no heavy equipment and move quickly so as to be under cover from the swarms of Russian columns by daybreak. The unit would then move back to Belgard, still held by the Germans, and then strike west for the German lines.

Fenet's I/RM moved off on time as planned, and then everything began to fall apart fast. De Bourmont's Régiment de Reserve had enormous trouble mustering and then moved far too slowly out of Körlin and back to Belgard. Order, counter-order and confusion followed and the entire Régiment began to break up. The more experienced NCOs voted with their feet and led their sections away into the mist, preferring to take their chances on their own and not in the utter disorganisation of the shredding column. As for Fenet he didn't look back. He and his battalion were soon way ahead of the rest of the Division and heading west. With Krukenberg accompanying them, Fenet led his battalion on an odyssey trying to rejoin the German lines, avoiding fire fights whenever possible until eventually they met up with German troops at Meseritz.

Dawn broke on 5 March and the gathering light found Puaud, de Bourmont and most of the Régiment de Reserve in a sorry state. Cold, tired, hungry and disorientated they were not in any kind of cover and were bunched dangerously close together. They were also hideously exposed trying to cross the flat and open plain to the south-west of Belgard having not moved far or fast enough to find the forests they so desperately needed to hide in when daylight came. The morning fog then lifted and only a few hundred metres away from the dishevelled Frenchmen were columns of Soviet tanks, artillery and infantry heading north and west. The Russians looked on with amazement at the sight that met their eyes, hundreds and hundreds of bedraggled men in the field grey of the enemy, out in the open with no armour and few weapons, and slowly tramping along in the field adjoining the road. The Russians reacted with glee and began to pour fire into the helpless ranks of SS men.

The column broke and men scattered, but it was too late. Rows of T-34s chased groups of fleeing grenadiers down, machine-gunning them and pulping survivors under their squealing tracks. It was shooting fish in a barrel! The Frenchmen had no anti-tank guns, and some didn't even have personal firearms with which to try to fight off the swarms of Soviets. Groups of Russian infantry ran amok shooting everything that moved and soon the plain was covered in dead and dying French SS men. It was a terrible slaughter and in less than an hour over 500 men from Charlemagne were either dead or prisoners of war. Prominent among the dead were the Division's Commander Edgar Puaud and the commander of the Régiment de Reserve, Victor de Bourmont. Some men did escape the carnage and amazingly managed to join up with Fenet's I/RM at Meseritz the following day, whilst others even turned up on the Oder to rejoin the German forces, but for most the plain of Belgard was the end of the line and they either died there, or began a long journey into Russian captivity.

II/RM and the end at Körlin

Bassompierre's part in the break-out plan was for his men to act as a rearguard and stay in Körlin to delay the Red Army. They were then to withdraw and follow on behind the rest of the Division. This was a truly difficult operation to conduct, to try to disengage from the enemy in contact and move swiftly to rejoin a column that they were not in physical contact with. But first came the delaying battle, and this part the French SS men played to perfection.

With fewer than 800 men Bassompierre conducted a vigorous and aggressive defence of the town for more than a day and a night. The Soviets were determined to take Körlin and open up its roads for the transit of their advancing columns, and so they sent in assault after assault of T-34s supported by wave upon wave of screaming infantry. Again the miracle weapon that was the panzerfäust came to the rescue of the Charlemagne men, as they brewed up tank after tank on the approach bridges and in the town itself. Well-sited machine guns butchered the Red infantrymen as they struggled forward through the smoking rubble and Soviet casualties were soon enormous.

As at Elsenau the town cemetery in Körlin became a focus for the defence with the Soviets pouring everything into taking it. In reply

Waffen-Hauptscharführer Eric Walter led his company into a savage counter-attack that came down to the bayonet. The Russians were thrown out of the cemetery but were soon back with even more men and tanks. In between concerted attacks the Soviets used the full weight of their artillery on the town. Shells and rockets from the deadly Stalin's Organs, *Katyushas*, rained down on the hapless French grenadiers in their makeshift positions. Many of the defenders were simply blown apart in the firestorm that engulfed the town and set it ablaze from end to end. Under cover of this curtain of explosive and shrapnel the inexhaustible Russians came on again, and once more were met by their French SS adversaries. Back in the cemetery Walter's remaining men were pushed back, but they counter-attacked again with Eric Walter leading as always, firing his machine gun from the hip. But Bassompierre knew this couldn't go on much longer. The fighting was now house-to-house, and the Frenchmen weren't strong enough to clear out the infiltrating Russians from the town's suburbs. Slowly they fell back, contesting every room, roof and garden path, but survival now lay in escape; the defence was over.

Bassompierre gathered his remaining officers and ordered a break out for nightfall on 6 March. It wasn't a moment too soon. The ammunition was now almost gone and the remaining grenadiers were at the end of their tether. They had been fighting for almost forty-eight hours in the blackened and burning ruins of Körlin with little food or water, and under constant bombardment and attack. The column formed up as night fell and prepared for a silent withdrawal. Unfortunately they had to leave their badly wounded comrades behind; only those who could walk could get out. A few hardy medics volunteered to stay behind with them, and they were joined by some diehard souls who volunteered to stay behind to man the guns and keep the Russians busy while the rest of the battalion slipped out of the town.

Led by Yves Rigeade and his company, the French SS men ghosted through the Soviet lines, most of the Russians they passed being asleep. Any Russian they met who was awake was silently killed, and then the French moved on. There was an occasional fire fight with the odd Soviet patrol, but by then the column was far from the burning pyre that was Körlin, and they were paid no attention. The break-out was a stunning success. Bassompierre had managed to somehow extricate his men from the hell of Körlin before the Russians realised what was going on and put in a final assault. They now had to rejoin the German lines. The problem was that no one was sure where those lines were exactly. In fact, getting out of Körlin was the least of the worries for the exhausted French battalion.

The men were not in a good physical shape, many carrying minor wounds that were untreated, with very little food or water, and they were soon reduced to sucking handfuls of snow. The weather was appalling with temperatures that stubbornly refused to crawl above zero degrees.

The winds were strong, increasing the bitter cold, and the snow kept falling onto the already numbed grenadiers. Maps and compasses were like gold dust, so that if the column was split up there was little hope of the men being able to find their way west, particularly as they had to avoid roads and tracks, travel cross country and at night in order to avoid the Red Army. Their only hope was to stay together and avoid contact with the roving Russian patrols. If they did that there was a slim chance they would make it back to the safety of their own lines.

That first night the battalion made good progress and dawn found them in a wood far away from Körlin. Here they rested for the day, but it was miserable for the SS men as they lay huddled together for warmth in their wet uniforms, unable to light fires to get dry or heat food, and they lay in shivering silence waiting for nightfall. Finally it began to get dark and Bassompierre led his men on the next leg of their escape. This though was to be the beginning of the end for the II/RM. The battalion came into contact with large numbers of Russian troops and began to break up. The French were forced to fight a series of running engagements through the woods, fields and tracks of Pomerania, twisting and turning first east then west, and finally in every direction to try to shake off the Russians. At every step men were shredding from the column. Many simply disappeared, either killed in fire fights, captured by roving Russian cavalry or, just too tired to go on they sat down in the snow and quietly froze to death. It took several days, but in the end the entire battalion that had fought on so bravely in Körlin, and who had managed to escape right under the noses of the Red Army, just fell apart. Groups and individuals wandered about the countryside for days, and even weeks, until they were either captured or went down fighting as they were finally cornered.

Waffen-Hauptscharführer Eric Walter, whose heroics in holding the cemetery in Körlin had frustrated the Soviets for so long, died attacking a Russian tank. Also killed were Waffen-Obersturmführer Français and the ex-commander of I/RR, Waffen-Hauptsturmführer Emile Monneuse. Monneuse had managed to get himself and his men out of the earlier encirclement at Bärenwalde but his luck finally ran out after Körlin. Bassomperre himself was captured, as were Rigeade, Girard, Gobion and de Perricot. Although as testament to the fortitude of the escapees, Gobion was only captured on the banks of the Oder on 24 March, over two weeks after breaking out of Körlin. One group from II/RM wasn't captured until 2 May, just six days before the end of the war! It was a tragic end for Bassompierre and the II/RM. They had fought so bravely in Körlin, but in so doing had left themselves with little hope of escape, their fate was that of many Wehrmacht units left behind the advancing Soviets and crushed to death in the snows of eastern Germany.

Frenchmen all over

With the destruction of Bassompierre's II/RM and the entire Régiment de Reserve, the Charlemagne had effectively ceased to exist as a Division. However, its time fighting in the frozen wastes of Pomerania was far from over, and a lot more French SS grenadiers were to die before the end of this bloody campaign.

There were now three major groupings of Charlemagne; the first was Fenet's I/RM, joined by associated stragglers, sitting in Meseritz after withdrawing from Körlin. The second was a battalion strength unit headed by Waffen-Hauptsturmführer Havette, the head of Charlemagne's artillery group, in the port of Kolberg, and lastly there was another battalion strength unit in the port city of Danzig. This unit was led by Waffen-Hauptsturmführer Obitz and included de Brangelin, Fatin and Matrin and several hundred men who had escaped from the battle in Elsenau. As well as these strong units there were hundreds of French SS grenadiers from all parts of the Division scattered in groups of various sizes, down to single men, over the whole of the Pomeranian battlefield. The fate of these Frenchmen was varied; many were captured half-starved and wounded in the fields, woods and farms that dotted the countryside. Many were killed fighting small, bitter battles with Russian patrols, and the fate of so many others is unknown; they simply disappeared in the maelstrom of war and were never heard of again.

Fenet

The I/RM, Krukenberg and various groups of Charlemagne all ended up at the mustering point of Meseritz. From here they joined the general German forces' disjointed and confusing withdrawal to the sea, in an attempt to reach a port and be saved by water. As with all the fleeing German forces, the French underwent a series of marches, counter-marches and twists and turns until they finally reached the Baltic at the small village of Horst late on the evening of 9 March. From here they were tasked with leading a breakthrough along the coast to get out of Pomerania. Part of their task was to escort a column, thousands strong, of German refugees desperately trying to flee the Soviet advance. Led by Krukenberg and Fenet, the pitiful column set off west along the beach and the adjacent coast road on the night of 11 March. The Frenchmen came up against a whole series of Soviet blocking forces as they struggled slowly on towards salvation. In the mass of tightly packed refugees the constant mortar and machine gun fire from Russian positions caused absolute mayhem, and the dead and wounded lay in heaps. Again and again it was down to the French SS grenadiers to charge forward and clear out another nest of Russian soldiers pouring fire into the would-be escapers. Grenadier after grenadier went down in the sand as Fenet, Roy and Krukenberg led their men in close quarter assault after assault to batter a way through the encroaching Soviets. Throughout the night and into the next day the column continued to forge onwards, not daring to stop. To stop was to die. It was a horrific experience for all. Gilbert Gilles, serving in the 1st Platoon of the 1st Company remembers:

> ...we came to a small cliff where an atrocious spectacle awaited us. Hundreds of corpses of women and children were on the beach. A refugee column, surprised by the Soviet arrival. We were immobile looking at those mutilated and naked corpses. Those young girls, mothers and grandmothers had been chain raped one or two days ago by the winners. Then their throats were cut and their bellies opened...

Late on in the afternoon of 12 March the survivors came to the bridge over the Oder river at Dievenow. On crossing it they were finally out of Pomerania.

Danzig

Those Frenchmen who had washed up in Danzig as they retreated northwards were placed under the command of Obitz and were formed into an alarm battalion, a unit designation the Germans used for hastily scraped together troops pressed into immediate service in times of crisis. Their orders were clear, dig in and protect the port city. For the best part of three weeks there was little activity beyond the occasional recce patrol by either side. Day by day the situation normalised for the French SS grenadiers, and they began to recover from the trauma of the earlier fighting on the railway line and at Elsenau. But this period of relative calm was bound not to last, and it all came to an end on 1 April 1945, when a major Red Army attack smashed through Danzig's outer defences and hit the weak French line full on. As was usual for the Soviets the attack was pre-empted by a massive artillery bombardment that shook the earth and smashed dugouts and trenches to bits. The end of the barrage brought no respite as behind the storm of steel came the armoured juggernaut of the assault. As ever the Frenchmen had little in the way of heavy weapons with which to combat the mass of attacking Soviet armour, but with the help of three Tiger tanks from another neighbouring German unit, they managed somehow to fight off the Russian onslaught. That one assault had caused crippling casualties, and along with the rest of the city's defenders the surviving Charlemagne men were evacuated by ship to Denmark, arriving in Copenhagen on 5 April.

Kolberg

Hundreds of Frenchmen managed to reach the port city of Kolberg after the battle at Elsenau. They included the remnants of the Compagnie d'Honneur, and once in the city they were incorporated as part of its defence force to resist the inevitable Soviet attacks. Although many of the French SS men were wounded or completely dispirited, they were formed into a makeshift unit and deployed to hold the perimeter until all the civilians in the city, both refugees and inhabitants, could be embarked by the Kriegsmarine and taken to safety farther west. Unlike their comrades in Danzig there was no rest for the Kolberg defenders, and they found themselves under attack by strong Soviet forces straightaway. Day after day the Russians and their Polish allies poured artillery and rocket fire into the ever dwindling perimeter, and then columns of tanks and accompanying infantry would advance firing point blank into the defenders' positions. The garrison would reply with withering small arms and panzerfäust fire, and sometimes even with naval gunfire support from offshore Kriegsmarine destroyers. This naval gunfire was particularly effective at smashing the Soviet assaults into bloody ruin, and day after day the Russians were sent reeling back. André Bayle, who fought at Kolberg, wrote of the siege:

> What strikes me is the extraordinary beating of the artillery, of the rocket launchers and the aeroplanes, but also the proliferation of the infantry, their acrobatic agility for heaving themselves onto the roofs, their automatic weapons which they fire in excess without a thought to the ammunition they use, and the snipers who take aim with great precision without being seen.
>
> Only towards the end shall we discover the plethora of tanks. We hopelessly resist, first from house to house, then from ruin to ruin, and finally from cellar to cellar, day and night, without respite. The enemy get some relief from duty, but not us!

As at Elsenau and Körlin, the cemetery in Kolberg became a focus of the defence and was bitterly contested by both sides. But in the end, as everywhere else in Pomerania, the strength of the Red Army soon told and street by street the stubborn defenders were pushed back to the sea. At last the evacuation of some 85,000 civilians was completed on the night of 15 March and the few remaining defenders embarked on the last of the ships for the relative safety of the west. For the French SS grenadiers the fighting had been ruinous, and a bare handful made it alive out of the city.

Postscript to Pomerania

Charlemagne had been brought to battle piecemeal in Pomerania, and was unable to concentrate its forces and familiarise itself with either the terrain or the enemy before being committed to action. Crucially it was not able to marry up with its integral heavy weapons that would have been vital in trying to combat massed artillery and tanks, let alone the huge weight of Soviet infantry numbers. It lacked everything but the most basic transport and so was condemned to foot slog around in the snows of north-eastern Germany when their enemies were either truck or armour-borne. Basic military necessities such as maps and compasses were only issued down to battalion level if at all, and most telling, there was a constant shortage of ammunition of all types. Even had there been sufficient ammunition the French lacked the transport to get it up to their forward troops. In these circumstances the ability of Charlemagne to effect anything other than local successes was nil. Where the SS men were able to place themselves in the face of the Soviet advance they fought well and consistently. Here their inability to manoeuvre was negated by the Russian need to overwhelm them, and so at the railway line, at Elsenau, Körlin, Danzig and Kolberg the men of Charlemagne did not disgrace themselves. Pomerania was a milestone for Charlemagne and its Frenchmen. Although still in total fewer than 8,000 men, the fighting in Pomerania involved by far the largest concentration of Frenchmen that would ever come together to fight in German uniform.

But the plaudits the Division received were hard won in Pomerania; the butcher's bill for the campaign was very high. One look at the command roster paints the picture. Among the casualties were the Divisional Commander, Puaud who was killed along with one of the Regimental Commanders, de Bourmont, and the other, Raybaud, was wounded. The Divisional Chief-of Staff, de Vaugelas, was captured. Of the eventual five men to hold battalion command, two were killed, two were wounded and one was captured. Among the company commanders two were killed, three wounded and three captured. Down at platoon level and below the losses in the ranks of the commanders were even higher. Whole sub-units of the Charlemagne had ceased to exist; the entire Régiment de Reserve and the II/RM formed at Körlin were wiped out. Those sub-units that did survive with some sort of cohesion were much reduced, and would never properly recover. It is difficult to get any accurate figures on total casualties for the Division due to the splintering of Charlemagne during the campaign and the subsequent disintegration of the Third Reich, but it is safe to assume a total casualty figure of over 5,000 men, with a high proportion being killed, maybe as many as 3,500. This represents almost fifty percent of the entire Divisional strength. As for equipment the Division was down to rifles, panzerfäusts and machine guns; everything else was gone.

Names to remember

Henri Fenet built on his reputation from Galicia of being one of the finest French SS commanders. His leadership of first the I/57 and then the I/RM was a resounding success. He managed to keep his troops together, cohesive and fighting all the way until they crossed the Oder out of Pomerania. His leadership was cool, calm and whenever necessary, vicious. In recognition of his successful campaign Fenet was promoted to Waffen-Hauptsturmführer.

Pierre Rostaing had survived. This was indeed an achievement considering he was involved in the slaughter on the plain of Belgard. By his own account, when the firing began, he ran like a man possessed to avoid death or capture. Unlike so many of his old comrades from the LVF, Rostaing managed to get himself out of the Soviet noose in Pomerania and back to the muster point at Carpin. With the deaths of so many he was now the most decorated Frenchmen still serving with the German armed forces.

André Bayle gave up command of 'his' platoon after Galicia and reverted to being a platoon NCO for Pomerania. He fought well and consistently and took part in all the major battles until finding himself bottled up in Kolberg during the Soviet siege. Along with his comrades, Bayle kept the Russians at bay in the bitter street fighting in the port town. He was awarded the Iron Cross 1st Class for his bravery in the defence, but it wasn't enough to get him out of the final collapse and, exhausted, cold and hungry André Bayle became a Soviet prisoner-of-war on the fall of the city. He wrote of his capture;

> On the 15th we take the risk of crossing the roads which are full of enemy tanks and soldiers who, surprisingly, shoot too late, giving us the possibility of catching up with around a hundred Germans who are sheltering under a protective porch. Successive groups attempt to escape, but are made into mincemeat by the hail of enemy bullets before our eyes. Some of those in my platoon, having found a civilian clothes shop, abandon their uniforms and try, unsuccessfully, to escape over the roofs. I remain with the others, but the German officers suddenly decide to raise the white flag. Here we are, stupidly trapped with them.
> Hands up!
> It's the rule of the game!
> It was the end for me!

Still only 18 years old, he then underwent an odyssey of survival as he, and so many of his fellows, were transported east to the horrors of the Soviet gulags. Bayle went first to the camp at Vladimir, then Tambow, and finally Novossibirsk, and in all the camps he saw so many of his comrades die of maltreatment and disease. Of some 100 Charlemagne prisoners with Bayle, fifty-two died in less than a year from malnourishment, dysentery or pneumonia. Eventually he was released and repatriated to France after the end of the war, where he was welcomed back with a trial in Valenciennes for his wartime service. André Bayle's shooting war was over, but not his struggle for survival. He would take no part in the last act, the Battle for Berlin.

CHAPTER X

Götterdämmerung in Berlin:
The End of Days

Orders were sent to concentrate all the surviving Frenchmen at Carpin in the wooded fastnesses of Mecklenburg. For those ragged and bloody men ordered to regroup south of Berlin they could look back proudly on their record in Pomerania. But the reality was that the 33rd Waffen-Grenadier-Division der SS Charlemagne (französische Nr.1) was utterly and totally shattered.

Although never at full established Wehrmacht divisional strength, the Charlemagne was still a considerable force of some 8,000 men when it deployed to Pomerania in February 1945. Come April barely 1,100 survivors could be mustered at the Divisional regrouping point. Among those missing from the thinned ranks were the majority of Charlemagne's officers and huge swathes of men from the old LVF and SS-Sturmbrigade Frankreich; for so many the fight in Pomerania had been their last. In reality a strong brigade strength unit in February, the Charlemagne could now not even man two rifle battalions. Also a straight headcount was not adequate to assess the battered condition of the few survivors. The hell they had endured in the snows of Pomerania had left its mark on the volunteers. Many of those who had survived physically were not what they had been mentally. The experience of continual massive Russian onslaughts, and then long and ignominious retreat through the terrible winter conditions of Pomerania, had ruined the spirit of many a soldier in the Division. It must be remembered that large numbers of the Frenchmen enlisted in the Division were not committed volunteers, but transfers from the NSKK, the Organisation Todt or the Kriegsmarine. Problems in the ranks were not limited to former members of these services either, for some former LVF men Pomerania was one campaign too far. Some ex-legionnaires had been fighting in the East since the winter of 1941–2, and the strain cannot be overstated. For some now standing in the much depleted ranks, Pomerania would be their last battle, even though they had survived the conflagration.

The future of Charlemagne
In the dying months of World War II the Germans desperately sought to stave off defeat by creating, almost on a whim, hosts of new and grandiose formations which they believed would hurl the Red Army back onto the steppes. Units such as the 32nd SS Freiwilligen-Grenadier-Division 30 Januar, the 35th SS Polizei-Grenadier-Division or the 38th SS Grenadier-Division Nibelungen, were made up of any and all available manpower. Barely equipped and hugely under strength these formations never even reached regimental, let alone divisional, size and had no military impact on the Front. All of the named divisions, and many more, disappeared into the Soviet maelstrom before they were even properly established. Yet it was not to be Charlemagne's fate to be swept up in the steamroller Soviet advance and disappear from history as so many of these later Waffen-SS divisions did. Charlemagne was to be no Lützow or Nibelungen; there was a final chapter waiting to be written by the exhausted men at Carpin.

War situation post-Pomerania
Nazi Germany's 'grand strategy' in the war was a conspicuous failure. The invasion of Soviet Russia while Britain was still undefeated, an unnecessary declaration of war on the sleeping United States behemoth, all these were symptomatic of a lack of consistency and focus on Nazi Germany's war aims. However, so often in the preceding years of the war Germany had defeated its enemies with superior 'campaign strategy', tactical analysis and decisive action. The 1940 Ardennes Offensive that had doomed the Western Allies to defeat, the encirclement and envelopment battles in White Russia and the Ukraine in 1941 that had seen over a million Soviet soldiers captured, are classic examples. However, as the war came to its bloody close in 1945 this acumen seemed to desert German military thinking.

The fast shrinking Nazi empire was under attack from almost all sides, but to vastly differing degrees. No one for instance would seriously have suggested that the main Allied danger would come across the Alps from Italy. For the Western Allies in particular the Ardennes Offensive of 1944–5 had bred caution into their commanders, as well as an appreciation of the obstacles still to face in crossing the Rhine and fighting through Germany's industrial heartland of the Ruhr. So for the Western Allies there was no quick route to victory, Montgomery's defeat at Arnhem had seen to that. That left the overwhelming threat to Germany from the East. The Red Army had been advancing continuously for over eighteen months, and had not tasted anything other than local defeat in all that time. 1944 especially had been the year of the Red Army with the celebrated '*Year of the Ten Victories*', that had seen it liberate almost its entire home territory, conquer Rumania, Bulgaria and most of Poland and grind the once all-conquering German military machine into bloody pieces. Now Hungary was almost totally occupied, and the road to the Balkans and Austria was almost in their grasp. Stalin was now definitely fighting the war with one eye firmly on the looming post-war settlement. Possession being nine-tenths of the law in international diplomacy, he was determined that Soviet soldiers would advance as far and fast as possible before the guns fell silent in Europe. However, this strategic necessity was balanced with Stalin's thirst for vengeance, and that obsessive need would only be assuaged by the taking of the German capital and the final destruction of his nemesis, Adolf Hitler.

Son of Georgia

Stalin is rightfully remembered as a monster, but beside that knowledge there is also an appreciation of his political skills. He was able to navigate the political alleyways of communist Russia so that he succeeded Lenin as supreme leader ahead of more able rivals such as Trotsky, and then lead the country for thirty years through huge turmoil and upheaval until his death in 1953.

This is all true, but what is sometimes forgotten in this retrospective on Stalin is that in his soul he was still Joseph Vissarionovic Djugashvili, a Georgian son of the soil from a land not unlike Sicily in its attachment to the way of the blood feud, the vendetta. In Georgia's rugged mountains and clannish communities, blood feuds lasted generations and a slight once given was never forgotten. For Stalin the vendetta with Hitler was in his blood. Stalin was incredibly paranoid about losing power, and it was Hitler who had come closest to making that fear a reality, in return the Soviet dictator would not rest until the Nazi Führer was dead. At the beginning of spring 1945 the two objectives most craved by Stalin were then one and the same: destroy Berlin and with it, Adolf Hitler. To add to this background information on Soviet intentions German intelligence itself in Fremde Heere Ost, Enemy Armies East, led by the elusive Colonel Reinhard Gehlen, was constantly feeding Hitler and OKW an accurate assessment of the massive Soviet build-up in the north of the Front. Another key indicator of Soviet intentions was that the Red forces being carefully brought together across the Oder were led by probably the two greatest Soviet commanders of the war, Zhukov and Koniev.

The Oder threat

Drawing these strands together the picture becomes clear. The main threat was obviously from the Soviets, and it would be from the northern sector, across the Oder, and aimed at taking Berlin and destroying Hitler personally. The failed German offensive Unternehmen Wacht am Rhein (Operation Watch on the Rhine), had seen Nazi Germany's last offensive reserves bled white in the winter snows of the Ardennes, but there were still considerable forces left with which to battle the rising tide. These forces were not enough to win the war, nor even delay the outcome for long, but they were enough to decide how the end was to come. The obvious response to the Soviet threat was to concentrate all remaining available forces to meet this threat, and in particular to bring together the Waffen-SS elites, who Hitler still believed could bring him a miracle. Hitler did indeed summon his praetorians, not for Berlin, but for Hungary. Sepp Dietrich and his 6th SS Panzer Army, consisting of the 1st Leibstandarte, 2nd Das Reich, 9th Hohenstaufen and 12th Hitlerjugend, powerful panzer divisions all, were wasted on the Hungarian plains. Indeed the majority of the Waffen-SS, so assiduously created by Himmler over years of intrigue and bloodshed, faced the end away from the main battle Fronts and played no part in the final defence of their Reich's capital and leader, strange indeed given their history and position as Hitler's personal guard and the ideological defenders of Nazism.

Berlin's defenders

As it was, the defence of Hitler and Berlin lay in the hands of two under strength Army divisions of LVII Corps, some Luftwaffe, and even Kriegsmarine field formations, and from the Waffen-SS there were only three formations, not one of which was German. First was the most powerful, the 11th SS Freiwilligen-Panzergrenadier-Division Nordland. Part of Felix Steiner's celebrated 3rd Germanisches SS Panzer Corps, that had held out so valiantly on the Narva, Brigadeführer Joachim Ziegler's Nordland Division was a shadow of its former self. Its armoured component was down to around fifty vehicles, concentrated mainly in the Hermann von Salza Panzer Battalion and the reconnaissance battalion, while in manpower terms it had suffered horribly in Courland and the earlier Oder battles. Total casualties since the beginning of 1945 had been just under 15,000, with over 4,500 of those being killed or missing. Such casualties could not be replaced at this stage of the war, and so the Nordland Division that was ordered to move to Berlin at midday on 17 April 1945 was barely a brigade in strength, let alone a powerful panzer grenadier division. In composition the Nordland Division was a 'classic Aryan' unit, being made up of volunteers from Norway, Denmark, Sweden and Switzerland among others. It had an excellent combat record, and as a mark of its quality, its members had been awarded a total of twenty-five Knight's Crosses for bravery, and this in only a single year since its creation in spring 1944. This tally of Knight's Cross awards was second only to the Wiking Division total, in terms of the non-German Waffen-SS divisions, and of course Wiking was not only acknowledged as the best of the foreign Waffen-SS divisions, but had also been in existence for far longer than any other foreign unit. Nordland then would play a huge part in the fighting to come; its armour, experience and general quality would mark it out as a mainstay of the defence.

Secondly there was a contingent of Latvians from the 15th Waffen-Grenadier-Division der SS (lettische Nr.1). Formed in February 1943, this Division was considered an excellent fighting formation, as indeed were all three Baltic Waffen-SS divisions, and the Latvians had been rewarded with a total of three Knight's Crosses. The Balts were not huge in number; much of their strength had been lost on the Narva and in the battles to protect their homelands. They were not an armoured formation either, so they lacked the heavy weaponry to combat the masses of Soviet tanks on equal terms. However they were determined and experienced, and had nothing to lose now their native land was under Soviet occupation. Both Nordland, and the 15th SS Grenadiers, also included numbers of Estonians in their ranks to further increase the multinational flavour of the defenders of Berlin.

Lastly there was the tattered, but still proud, remnants of the 33rd Waffen-Grenadier-Division der SS Charlemagne (französische Nr.1). Though smaller in number than the ranks of the Nordland, and like the Balts possessing no armoured vehicles or heavy weapons, in so many ways the Battle for Berlin was to be their story, Charlemagne's story.

No Stalingrad here

The Battle for Berlin was to be, in many ways, an extraordinary confrontation.

For almost six years, armies of millions of men and tens of thousands of vehicles had fought across a landscape of hundreds of thousands of square kilometres, ranging from the English Channel to the gates of Moscow, and from the deserts of North Africa to the frozen wastes of Norway and Lapland. Decisive clashes such as El Alamein, Stalingrad, Kursk and Normandy had been the focus of titanic struggles with both sides straining every military sinew to win. Huge forces commanded by legendary generals had been the norm; Rommel's Afrika Korps/Italian army versus Montgomery's Eighth Army at El Alamein; Model, Hausser and Hoth with Germany's entire armoured strength against Rokossovsky and Vatutin's eleven Soviet armies at Kursk. Yet at the end, at the very end, at Hitler's vaunted Götterdämmerung, the twilight of the gods, in Berlin, the end of the world, where was the final showdown to end all showdowns? In modern parlance, where was the 'mother of all battles'? The Soviets were ready to play their part for sure. Stalin had lined up Zhukov and Koniev, his ablest leaders, commanding a huge mass of Soviet Russia's finest. The Red Armies facing Berlin were truly terrifying in their sheer scale, over two-and-a-half million men, 41,600 guns and mortars, 6,250 tanks and self-propelled guns and 7,500 aircraft. To put that in some sort of context the Wehrmacht had had only 3,580 tanks and self-propelled guns and 1,830 aircraft to invade the whole of Russia at the beginning of Operation Barbarossa less than four years earlier. At this stage even those sorts of numbers were a pipe dream for Germany, the defenders were barely a fraction of the Red tide. This was to be no contest in any real military sense, but neither was it to be a walkover. For Stalin then the stage was set, the actors in place, it was merely waiting for curtain-up.

But on the Nazi side the picture couldn't have been more different. The Reichsminister for Propaganda, Joseph Goebbels, had consistently stated: 'The National Socialists will either win together in Berlin or die together in Berlin.'

Goebbels was also Gauleiter, Nazi Party governor, of Berlin, and as such would be perhaps expected to place huge emphasis on the military position of the capital, but he was not the only one who considered Berlin to be of paramount importance, Marx had said: '…whoever possesses Berlin possesses Germany, and whoever controls Germany, controls Europe.'

Stalin undoubtedly knew the quote, and it is inconceivable that Hitler hadn't heard it, and yet Goebbels' Nazi rhetoric was totally removed from the military reality. If the Nazi leadership regarded the holding of Berlin as so important, then where was the force with which to defend the capital? Where were Germany's last legions and her finest leaders? After six years of monumental conflict Nazi Germany still possessed a powerful military machine with numbers of battle hardened veterans and some of the finest commanders of the 20th century. Where were the Mansteins, the Haussers and von Runstedts, where were the tattered remnants of Nazi Germany's famed Wehrmacht, and of course the National Socialists' very own political soldiers, the Waffen-SS? At every other decisive juncture of the war both sides had brought everything to bear that they possibly could in order to win, and yet now the Nazis seemed blinded to what was happening.

The praetorians defend Austria, and not Berlin

As the Soviet juggernaut steamed towards Berlin the bizarre situation was created whereby the overwhelming bulk of the German Waffen-SS was defending Austria in the south, while Hitler and much of the Nazi Party hierarchy was in Berlin and the north, and being defended by little more than a handful of Germans and foreigners. The defenders of Berlin could barely muster 100,000 men and 100 tanks. This then was to be no

Stalingrad, no drama played out for weeks and weeks in the smouldering ruins of a once great city; rather this was to be a brief but bloody anti-climax. Nazi Germany's last stand, the final cataclysm, would be fought by a tiny fraction of her remaining formations, and by commanders, such as Weidling and Krukenberg, competent commanders to be sure, but whose names did not exactly cry out from the annals of German military success during the preceding war years. This then was the scene that enabled the few men of Charlemagne to make such a statement of defiance, the few against the many. It was never going to be a battle for victory, it was to be hopeless and forlorn, but nevertheless a battle that thousands of men thought worth fighting. That fact alone makes the Battle for Berlin significant.

But before the Battle for Berlin there would come the reformation and resurrection of the Charlemagne Division.

Reorganisation

Charlemagne was to undergo two separate restructurings before it was committed to battle for the last time. Firstly the Division was reformed with three battalions, two of infantry and the third being support weapons. SS-Bataillon 57 was commanded by the newly-promoted Waffen-Hauptsturmführer Fenet, SS-Bataillon 58 by the Corsican ex-Milicien Waffen-Obersturmführer Géromini, and the anti-tank, flak and assault guns of the Heavy Battalion were commanded by Waffen-Sturmbannführer Boudet-Gheusi. As such the formation was now reduced to a much smaller and more appropriate regimental structure, but the Divisional designation was not abandoned and lived on, even if the formation itself was at a drastically reduced strength.

The strength of the unit gradually increased over the next few weeks as surviving stragglers from the fighting in Pomerania came in, supplemented by men returning from injury, and most significantly by those who had missed Pomerania altogether by virtue of their being away on various command and specialist training courses at the time.

In early April 1945 Himmler and Krukenberg agreed to improve the future combat effectiveness of the Division by ridding the swelling ranks of those whose hearts were no longer in it. These men were not Germans after all, and it was recognised that as foreign volunteers they had a right to opt out of the remaining conflict if they so wished. This was not done on some kind of sentimental whimsy from Himmler or Krukenberg, but as a cold calculation that by releasing those unwilling to carry on fighting, their equipment could be better used by other units. There was also a tacit recognition that perhaps not all of the original volunteers had been entirely willing in the first place. It was hoped as well that those who would now come forward to fight on to the bitter end would be a serious hard core of individuals who could be relied on in the last dark days to come. This calculation was to be proved entirely correct and a sound military decision. Krukenberg gave all the men the choice in front of them and awaited their decision. That choice was to continue to bear arms and fight on, or be disarmed and work as labourers in a Construction Battalion digging fortifications.

Unsurprisingly the entire Compagnie d'Honneur, already busy transforming themselves into a new incarnation as a Close Combat School to train the rest of the regiment in Weber's combat techniques, chose to fight on. They were joined by three-quarters of Fenet's SS-Bataillon 57 and half of Géromini's SS-Bataillon 58. But around 400 Frenchmen did decide enough was enough and gave up the fight. Command of these men was given to Waffen-Hauptsturmführer Roy who complained bitterly to Krukenberg about the decision. Roy wished to fight on but Krukenberg needed a reliable officer in charge of the Construction Battalion and Robert Roy was it. In a shock move Géromini was removed from command of SS-Bataillon 58 and made a company commander under Roy instead. This was the direct result of a serious personality clash with Krukenberg who saw the Corsican as a troublemaker. Many of those who opted out were former Miliciens who were totally unprepared for the butchery of the Eastern Front, and whose experiences in Pomerania had completely unnerved them. However the ex-Miliciens were joined by some former LVF legionnaires, and even a small sprinkling of ex-SS-Sturmbrigade men who were wrecked after Pomerania. For some ex-PPF party men the final straw came when news filtered through of the death of Jacques Doriot. He had survived combat on the Eastern Front when he served with the LVF, and attempted assassination by the Maquis back home in France, but on 22 February 1945 his luck finally ran out, and he was killed when his car was strafed by an Allied fighter plane near Sigmaringen. For some of his erstwhile followers it was the end of their dream and they would fight no more.

Of those who stayed, ex-LVF legionnaires and ex-SS-Sturmbrigade men made up the majority. They really were the hard core. Mostly the younger men and yet experienced combat veterans by now, they would not break or bend, and they would not give an inch.

The call to arms

The final Soviet offensive of the Second World War began on the morning of 16 April 1945. Zhukov's and Koniev's Fronts crashed through the German 9th and 4th Panzer Armies. Gaping holes were soon torn in the hugely under-strength German lines, and the Red Army raced almost unimpeded for Berlin. The last major obstacle to a direct attack on the city itself, the Seelow Heights, were captured by Zhukov's forces soon thereafter, but at the enormous cost of over 30,000 Soviet dead. Only now did it seem that Hitler woke up to the danger to Berlin, and orders went out to a host of units, both real and imagined, to either head for Berlin or prepare to counter-attack the Soviet pincers moving to encircle the capital.

During the night of 23–24 April 1945 Brigadeführer Krukenberg was awoken, at his Headquarters in Carpin, by a telephone call from Berlin. He was given a set of verbal orders. A telegram then arrived to confirm these instructions. Krukenberg himself was ordered to Berlin immediately to take over command of a division whose commander was being replaced through illness; this would turn out to be Joachim Ziegler of the Nordland. He was further ordered to form a Kampfgruppe from the remaining Charlemagne grenadiers and bring them with him to participate in the defence of the city.

Krukenberg called an O Group (Orders Group) of his officers in the castle at Carpin, and explained the situation to them. He told them that he only wanted willing men, volunteers, with him on this final journey, and asked his company commanders to speak to their men and gather all those still willing to fight on to be ready for a move to Berlin early the next day. The decision to take only volunteers was guided by several issues. Firstly Krukenberg was aware that even after the recent reorganisation, with the unwilling leaving for the Construction Battalion, there were still some who had taken a beating in Pomerania and had no further heart for the battle. Secondly, and more importantly, there were the pure logistical problems. There was not enough transport to take all of the Division to the capital, and not nearly enough weaponry to arm everyone even if they could get there.

Two of the assembled company commanders, Waffen-Untersturmführer Labourdette and Waffen-Obersturmführer Michel, paraded their companies of the SS-Bataillon 57 and asked them to take one pace forward if they wished to volunteer. To a man they did. SS-Obersturmführer Wilhelm Weber didn't even ask his men of the Compagnie d'Honneur, renamed the Kampfschule – the Close Combat School – to volunteer, but simply told them they were going to Berlin. Pierre Rostaing did the same; a senior NCO company commander, he told his men of the situation and asked if anyone didn't want to go. No one said a word. Rostaing's 6th Company was the only sub-unit from the SS-Bataillon 58 asked to join the Berlin-bound Kampfgruppe. The new unit was named the SS-Sturmbataillon Charlemagne, and was some 400 to 500 men strong. Overall command was given to none other than the redoubtable Henri Fenet. He had served with the original SS-Sturmbrigade Frankreich in Galicia, then had taken a full part in the horrors of Pomerania, and was now officer commanding the French SS bound for Berlin. With him he would take five companies; the 1st commanded by Labourdette, the 2nd by Michel, the 3rd by Rostaing, the 4th by Waffen-Oberscharführer Jean Ollivier, and lastly the Kampfschule under Weber, the only German officer in the new SS-Sturmbataillon.

These men of the SS-Sturmbataillon were the best of the remaining French SS grenadiers, all seasoned veterans of the Eastern Front, some with over three years' experience of fighting the Red Army already. The old SS-Sturmbrigade Frankreich veterans were the mainstay of the battalion, added to them were Rostaing's men, almost all ex-LVF to a man. These soldiers were the hard core, the hard wood of the French contribution to the Waffen-SS in World War II. None had any illusions about the outcome of the coming battle. They were going to Berlin to fight and die. Yet survivors talk of incredibly high morale among the volunteers as they assembled for their departure, of how they all felt that they would be part of history, and that part would be one of honour.

Twelve Luftwaffe trucks and a number of private cars were gathered to take the unit to Berlin, and in the meantime the volunteers grabbed every available weapon and round of ammunition they could find. Only Rostaing's men didn't now have one of the new *Sturmgewehr* 43 assault rifles each, but all the companies had an abundance of panzerfäusts, and at least one of the superb MG42 machine guns in each section.

The *Sturmgewehrs* would be invaluable in urban fighting. The name literally means 'assault rifle', and indeed they were the very first assault rifles produced. Able to fire accurate single shots, and also bring down the weight of fire of an automatic weapon, they were revolutionary. Captured in large numbers by the Red Army in the final months of the war, they formed the model for the ubiquitous AK47 after the war.

At 0830hrs on the morning of 24 April the convoy set off on the 100-kilometre or so journey to Berlin. It is difficult to imagine the chaos on the roads as hordes of fleeing German civilians joined with the flotsam of the defeated German Army to try to get to the west and out of the way of the advancing and vengeful Red Army. The French were swimming against this tide in trying to get into the capital, and the going was difficult and frustrating. The original plan to enter Berlin via Oranienburg was cancelled and several other routes were tried. Eventually Krukenberg found a route in through the fast closing Soviet pincers, but only after being strafed by a Soviet aircraft, having a bridge mistakenly blown up on them by nervous Volkssturm, and losing two trucks and the troops in them in the confusion. These disappointed men eventually turned up back at Carpin, where some of the remaining grenadiers there were waiting for more transport to arrive so they could be ferried into Berlin. But it was too late. The capital was surrounded and none could now get in. No one could get out either.

The Charlemagne convoy drove into Berlin from the north-west at Nauen, driving over the Havel river and the Heerstrasse, the old East–West axis of Berlin. They then drove on to the *Reichssportsfeld* in Charlottenburg, the 1936 Olympic Stadium, where they regrouped and stocked up on further weaponry and ammunition from a cache of supplies abandoned there by the Luftwaffe.

First orders

By now it was nightfall on the 24th and the Frenchmen posted sentries and got their heads down for some rest. Krukenberg meanwhile went with his adjutant, SS-Hauptsturmführer Pachur, to the Reichs Chancellery to report to General Krebs and the chief SS liaison officer, Herman Fegelein. There Krukenberg was briefed to report to General Weidling, who had been appointed Commandant of Berlin the day before. He was told his Frenchmen were destined for the district of Neukölln to the east in the outer suburbs, where the Russians were still being held. As Krukenberg was receiving his instructions, the French SS men back at the *Reichssportsfeld* were woken for reveille, after which Fenet took stock of who had actually got through to Berlin and reorganised them ready for combat. He would remain in command with a small Headquarters staff. There would be four smaller rifle companies (nos. 1–4), each comprising around sixty to seventy men, as well as SS-Obersturmführer Weber's Kampfschule men. The total number of French SS grenadiers who got through was around 300. The SS-Sturmbataillon Charlemagne order of battle was as follows on 25 April 1945:

Battalion Commander : Waffen-Hauptsturmführer Henri Fenet (ex-Milice and SS-Sturmbrigade)

Orderly Officers : Waffen-Standartenoberjunkers Jacques Frantz (ex-SS- Sturmbrigade), Alfred Douroux (ex-LVF)

- 1st Company

Commander : Waffen-Untersturmführer Labourdette (ex-NSKK and SS-Sturmbrigade)

Assistants : Waffen-Standartenoberjunkers Jean Cossard (ex-LVF), Croisille (ex-SS-Sturmbrigade)

Platoon Commander : Waffen-Standartenoberjunker Boulmier (ex-LVF)

Platoon Commander : Waffen-Standartenoberjunker Maxime de Lacaze (ex-Milice)

Platoon Commander : Waffen-Standartenoberjunker Jacques Le Maignan de Kérnagat (ex-NSKK and SS-Sturmbrigade)

- 2nd Company
  Commander   : Waffen-Obersturmführer Pierre Michel
                           (ex-LVF and SS-Sturmbrigade)
  Platoon Commander   : Waffen-Oberscharführer Lardy (pseudonym,
                           ex-SS-Sturmbrigade)
  Platoon Commander   : Waffen-Standartenoberjunker Neroni
                           (ex-SS-Sturmbrigade)
  Platoon Commander   : Waffen-Oberscharführer Mongourd (ex-
                           Milice)

- 3rd Company
  Commander   : Waffen-Hauptscharführer Pierre Rostaing
                           (ex-LVF)
  Assistant   : Waffen-Standartenoberjunker Jean Dumoulin
                           (ex-LVF)
  Platoon Commander   : Waffen-Standartenoberjunker Jean Ginot
  Platoon Commander   : Waffen-Standartenoberjunker Gaston
                           Baumgartner (ex-LVF)

(3rd Platoon had been separated and forced to turn back)

- 4th Company
  Commander   : Waffen-Oberscharführer Jean Ollivier
                           (ex-SS-Sturmbrigade)
  Assistant   : Waffen-Standartenoberjunker Protopopoff
                           (ex-LVF, a White Russian who had made his
                           home in France)
  Platoon Commander   : Waffen-Unterscharführer Fieselbrand
  Platoon Commander   : Waffen-Standartenoberjunker Bellier
  Platoon Commander   : Sauvageot (rank unknown, ex-LVF)

- Kampfschule
  Commander   : SS-Obersturmführer Wilhelm Weber
                           (ex-SS Germania)
  Platoon Commander   : Waffen-Oberscharführer Pierre Bousquet
                           (ex-SS-Sturmbrigade)
  Platoon Commander   : Waffen-Unterscharführer Aimé-Blanc
  Platoon Commander   : Waffen-Unterscharführer Gerard Fontenay
                           (ex-SS-Sturmbrigade)

The reformed battalion then got back in its trucks in the morning and
headed east to Hasenheide in the newly-designated Defence Sector C,
which covered the south-west of the city. This sector had been assigned

to Weidling's most powerful combat formation, the 2,000 or so men of the Nordland. The Charlemagne were to join them and add some much needed combat power as an assault battalion, and Krukenberg was to take over Divisional command of Nordland from Ziegler. He would then report directly to Weidling. This then was Fenet's chain of command for the coming battle.

As the small convoy drove through the Berlin streets there was an unnatural quiet in the city. Civilians were still going to work, the S-Bahn was running, there was little or no evidence of troops or defences, and all that could be heard of the war was the steady rumble of artillery fire in the distance. This was stark evidence of the lack of preparedness of the city to face attack. Where were the strong points, trenches and tank obstacles? In reality they weren't there. Although declared a *Festung*, a fortress, months previously, there had been no serious effort to prepare a defence.

Fighting in built up areas, FIBUA in British Army parlance, is a specialist form of warfare that demands special skills from the troops involved in order to be successful. It is as much a speciality, in warfare terms, as fighting in forests, the jungle, deserts or the Arctic. Urban warfare can be truly horrific for an attacker; the advantages are almost all with the defender, and casualties for an assaulting force can be astronomical. Stalingrad had proved this beyond doubt. However, as any trained soldier knows, a successful urban defence requires two things above all: time and resources. Time is simple to quantify; every day that is devoted to a defence hugely increases its potency. As for resources, these include men and material. Put simply to resist large numbers of attackers requires large numbers of defenders. Those troops also require a range of defence stores and the necessary training and ingenuity to turn them into a variety of obstacles for infantry and armour that can be covered by both direct and indirect fire. Everything must also be closely coordinated and brought together into an overall defensive structure. That structure must include plans for counter-attacks, and have men at its disposal who have the determination and grit to see them through. On viewing the defences of Berlin, Krukenberg was not alone in concluding that almost every aspect needed for a successful, or even long-lasting, defence was missing. The only thing they did have was the commitment and calibre of the Charlemagne and Nordland troops.

First combat

The scene at Hasenheide when Krukenberg and the French SS grenadiers arrived was very different from the almost peacetime atmosphere pervading so much of the rest of the city. The Nordland's Headquarters had just been bombed by Soviet planes and confusion reigned. Krukenberg formally relieved Ziegler of command; the two generals actually knew each other, having served together in the Baltic states, and he was shocked to find out just how dire the situation was. The Nordland was now less than a weak regiment in strength, petrol stocks were very low and there was no sign of a coordinated defence in the sector. However, it was also obvious that this sector would not be the main axis of the Soviet assault. As such it was a military necessity to relocate both the Nordland and the SS-Sturmbataillon Charlemagne to a more central position from where they could counter the expected Soviet attack more effectively. Krukenberg requested that he make the necessary moves, and after permission was granted, moved his new Divisional Headquarters to the cellars of the Berlin Opera House on the afternoon of the 25th. This was to enable a defence of the central Sector Z, based on the Gendarmenmarkt in the city centre. In charge of this vital sector was a Luftwaffe Colonel, Seifert, based in the old Luftfahrtsministerium, the Air Ministry Building. Seifert was no fan of the Waffen-SS, and informed Krukenberg that neither he nor his men were welcome in the sector. Seifert further added that the positions he had emplaced were more than adequate for the defence of the area, and that he would prefer it if the Waffen-SS left! Krukenberg was flabbergasted. Even more so when a quick inspection proved that Seifert's claimed dispositions were illusory and that the sector was actually woefully unprepared.

By now the light was fading, and back in Hasenheide the Frenchmen were billeted for the night with preparatory orders for an attack on the Russian positions in Neukölln the next morning. That night the French SS sent out local patrols which claimed the first victories for the men of Charlemagne, when two men from Waffen-Oberscharführer Mongourd's platoon in 2nd Company, the 17-year-old grenadier, Jean-François Lapland, and his only slightly older section commander, Waffen-Unterscharführer Fodot, found and destroyed two Soviet tanks with panzerfäusts. The men had actually been separated from their patrol and on finding the enemy tanks had hidden behind a fence waiting for it to get dark enough to attack. It was around 0300hrs when they crept along the street to within range of the tanks. The effective range of a panzerfäust being what it was, they had to be close, and close they got, so close indeed they could both hear the crackling of one of the tanks' radio sets. The two SS men hardly dared to breathe so as to not wake the sleeping crews. Expecting any second to be challenged with a hail of gunfire, they slowly and carefully moved up to within almost spitting distance of the huge steel monsters. Both of them then carefully aimed the clumsy metal tubes, and fired. The blasts split the night, and the hollow charges of the panzerfäusts struck their targets and both tanks went up in flames. As a one-shot weapon, the empty panzerfäust tubes were then thrown away and the grenadiers ran as fast as they could back to their own lines. It would not be long before their next action, the French counter-attack was planned for daybreak on 26 April.

Battle in Neukölln

From the Neukölln town hall the French grenadiers were to attack along the Berlinerstrasse supported by some of Nordland's armour. This included two Panthers, a handful of Sturmgeschütz self-propelled guns and a mighty King Tiger. The King Tigers, the biggest ever tank produced in World War II and armed with the all-conquering 88mm gun, were from the SS Heavy Panzer Battalion 503 commanded by SS-Sturmbannführer Fritz Herzig. Like the Tigers before them, the King Tigers were grouped in these Heavy Battalions and then attached to a division for a specific operation. In an earlier action one of these tanks, commanded by SS-Hauptscharführer Karl Körner, came upon a mass of Soviet T-34 and Josef Stalin II heavy tanks being refuelled and re-armed on the Bollersdorf road. Körner, obviously a 'graduate' of the famous Michael Wittmann school of tank warfare, proceeded to shoot the lead and last tanks in the line, effectively trapping the rest. He then emptied his gun racks into the mass of armoured vehicles and drove back to the defence lines in Berlin. His tally for the day stood at over 100 tanks and twenty-six anti-tank guns destroyed, as well as a pile of soft-skinned vehicles. For this action he was awarded the Knight's Cross.

Fenet had seen his 1st Company detached to the Tempelhof sector on his right, so had only three companies available for the assault. He deployed them in the classic formation of two up with one in reserve. The lead companies were Michel's 2nd and Rostaing's 3rd, with Ollivier's 4th in reserve.

Rostaing's Company advanced down the Braunauerstrasse, parallel with Berlinerstrasse. The static King Tiger (it had almost no petrol) was in direct support. The Company came under mortar and anti-tank gun fire, as well as fire from Soviet T-34 tanks, and enemy infantry. In particular there was steady fire from snipers and machine-gun nests. The French SS grenadiers advanced with real élan, dashing forward from doorway to doorway, and clearing each house floor by floor, and room by room. Such fighting is exhausting, both physically and mentally. Toss a grenade into a room, wait for the blast and then into the room as fast as possible shooting anything that moves. It drains ammunition and nerves. In such combat there is no front or rear, the enemy can be anywhere and fire at you from any angle; it is true three-dimensional battle. As usual Rostaing led his men with aggression and calm authority, and was responsible himself for destroying one T-34 with a panzerfäust (although one of his men was

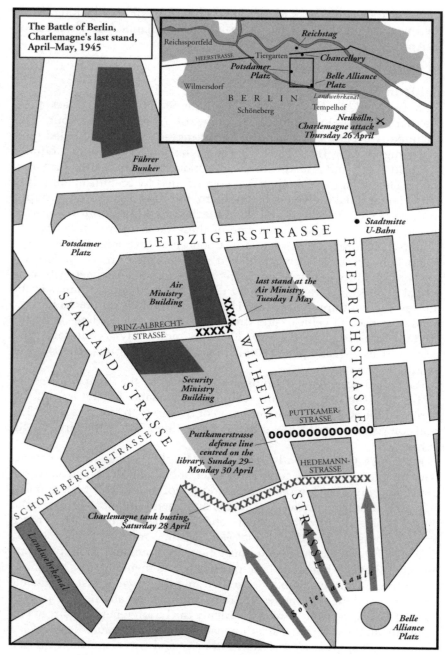

The Battle for Berlin, April–May 1945

decapitated by a piece of shrapnel from the blast as the tank exploded). The Company advance was a success, clearing the Russians all the way back to the Richard Platz, but casualties were heavy. Of his commanders alone, Rostaing lost Waffen-Oberjunkers Ginot and Baumgartner wounded, and Dumoulin was killed. One well-hidden Russian machine-gun nest killed nearly a dozen of his men before Rostaing shot the crew dead. In one hour the 3rd Company had lost one quarter of its strength.

Michel's 2nd Company did not fare as well. Attacking along Berlinerstrasse itself Michel had already lost Lardy's platoon on an earlier patrol prior to the attack; they were later surrounded and captured by the Russians. The Russian fire that met the advancing French grenadiers was very heavy. The advance pushed on but the Company Commander, Pierre Michel, was badly wounded almost at once, and soon the assault platoons had lost contact with each other and the momentum of the attack was gone. Michel was evacuated, but then disappeared. He almost certainly died of his wounds somewhere in the centre of Berlin during the final days of the battle.

Worst of all was the fate that befell the 4th Company back in battalion reserve. A salvo of artillery rounds caught the young French grenadiers out in the open and decimated the Company. Fifteen men were killed and a further dozen or so were wounded, including one platoon commander, Feiselbrand, and the Company Commander, Jean Ollivier. Fenet himself went to see the situation with the 4th Company, and found a scene of blood and confusion. Feiselbrand's men were amputating his right leg below the ankle, which was only just held on by a flap of skin.

The attack had been brief, bloody and a success. The Red Army were pushed back and suffered significant losses, but it was in vain. Back at the SS-Sturmbataillon Headquarters, Fenet had received an order from Divisional HQ instructing him to halt the attack. The overall situation had changed, and the Soviets had cracked open the city's defences in another sector, and were driving for the city centre. Fenet's companies were in grave danger of being outflanked, encircled and wiped out.

Hold on!

Weber's Kampfschule men were also detached to the Tempelhof sector, along with their comrades from the 1st Company, so that Fenet had just three under-strength companies to fight the defensive battle around the Neukölln town hall. Their flanks were open, contact having been lost with any friendly units on both sides, and the Soviet infantry started to infiltrate around the leading French platoons. The only bright spark was the fact that behind the Frenchmen their withdrawal route to Hermannplatz was still secure, so as long as that escape route remained clear the Charlemagne had a chance.

In the midst of all the fighting the French were unexpectedly reinforced by several hundred local Hitler Youth volunteers, the majority of whom were under 16 years old. Called to action by the rantings of Hitler and Goebbels, these boys were armed with nothing more than panzerfäusts and World War I Mauser rifles with a handful of rounds. Given a few hours' training in their weapons' use, and then sent into combat against the might of Zhukov's armies, it was nothing less than sheer murder. But alongside the experienced French SS grenadiers the Hitler Youth boys fought like demons. Too young to appreciate the dangers they faced, these children took absurd risks as they fired their clumsy, vintage bolt-action rifles at the well-armed Soviet infantry swarming towards them. On seeing a T-34 they would eagerly crawl forward and fire the clumsy panzerfäust tubes that were sometimes almost as big as them. It was appalling, but horrifyingly effective. Attack after attack was beaten off, even an armour heavy assault down Berlinerstrasse, which was crushed with the help of a Nordland Tiger tank. During the fighting Fenet was shot in the left foot, and the leader of his runners section, the 20-year-old SS-Sturmbrigade veteran Waffen-Rottenführer Millet, was killed. Millet had somehow managed to keep up communications with the fighting companies, but his luck had just run out. His place was taken by the 19-year-old Corsican, Roger Roberto.

Fenet continued to direct the defence from a chair! Eventually Red infantry got behind the Frenchmen and threatened to cut off any retreat towards Hermannplatz. In desperation Waffen-Oberjunker Douroux, from Battalion Headquarters, quickly grabbed any men he could find around the town hall and led them in a charge into the Russian positions to the rear. The fight was short and vicious. It came down to spades, knives and grenades, as the French grenadiers and the Hitler Youth children cleared room after room. It was too much for the Russians, and they ran.

Darkness was now beginning to fall, and the Charlemagne had been fighting in Neukölln since before dawn. Past 1900hrs Fenet received a report that Soviet tanks had finally outflanked him and were heading towards Hermannplatz. There was no time to lose, and the companies were mustered and withdrawn, without loss, back west towards Hermannplatz. Disengaging in contact is an extremely hazardous operation but the SS-Sturmbataillon had managed it, and just in time! Once back in the relative safety of their own lines the SS men and Hitler Youth boys linked up with a handful of Nordland's Sturmgeschütz and proceeded to ambush a column of Soviet armour, and soon almost forty enemy tanks were burning as the sun set over the smoke-wreathed district of Neukölln. But not all of the Charlemagne men got out though. From 2nd Company Waffen-Oberscharführer Mongourd's platoon, that of the intrepid tank busters of Lapland and Fodot, was cut off and forced to surrender. Only Lapland himself escaped. Mongourd was to survive the Battle for Berlin and Soviet captivity only to be tried, convicted and shot in Lyon in 1946 for his service as a commander with the Milice in the Limousin during the war.

Tempelhof and the 1st Company

As for Labourdette's Company they spent most of the day in reserve on the Tempelhof sector, and only went into action late in the afternoon. The Company was then hit by a wave of Russians who submerged it in their cries of '*Urrah!*' They managed to extricate themselves and hastily retreated to a local cemetery, and there fought a bloody holding action against huge numbers of enemy infantry. Late that night the Company was reunited with the rest of the SS-Sturmbataillon Charlemagne, only to be detached again under orders from the Sector Commander. Fenet protested vigorously; he wanted the last surviving French SS men to fight, and if necessary to die, together. This protest fell on deaf ears, and Fenet once gain said goodbye to Labourdette. 26 April had been a day of blood for the SS-Sturmbataillon Charlemagne. They had fought a messy battle of attack and counter-attack in Neukölln, and been engaged defending Tempelhof and its airfield. The butcher's bill was high. Labourdette's 1st Company was down to forty men, 2nd Company was the same having lost two entire platoons, Rostaing's 3rd Company was down to thirty survivors out of the original strength of eighty, and the 4th was even worse, having been reduced to a mere twenty men. Both the 2nd and the 4th Companies had lost their commanding officers. Half the battalion was already gone after one day's combat. But the Russians had paid a high price too. Neukölln was a nasty surprise for the Red Army. They did not anticipate concerted and heavy counter-attacks and had lost a host of infantrymen and dozens of tanks.

Back at the Chancellery, Krukenberg had finally persuaded General Weidling, in what turned out to be their last ever communication, to place him and the Nordland Division, along with the SS-Sturmbattaillon Charlemagne, in their own sector. This meant they would finally be out of Colonel Seifert's control, and would be able to make up for the total lack of preparations for the defence carried out by the Luftwaffe officer. Such was the capriciousness of war, boys and old men were being hanged all over the capital, by gangs of roving SS men, on the flimsiest evidence that they were deserting their posts. Yet here was an obviously incompetent officer putting the entire city's defence at risk by his negligence and negativity, and yet he was left in command of troops! The military mind sometimes has no rhyme or reason!

27 April: reorganisation

Friday dawned another hot and dusty day in Berlin. Krukenberg briefed all the Divisional officers, including Fenet, on the reorganisation, and then moved his Headquarters to the Stadtmitte U-Bahn station, where it was located in an old tramcar. The Nordland's Norge and Danmark panzer grenadier regiments were brought up into the line alongside the Charlemagne, who were now designated as specialist 'tank busters'. The remaining Nordland tanks, including the last eight runners from SS Heavy Panzer Battalion 503, were placed so as to be able to respond to any threat to the Front, and the Divisional artillery was also moved from the Tiergarten to a more suitable location to achieve the same result. All was relatively quiet with little more than heavy Russian artillery fire, and some local patrolling. Krukenberg used the calm to hold a solemn ceremony in the U-Bahn station where he awarded a host of Iron Crosses to French grenadiers who had fought bravely in the Neukölln battle. The morale of the SS-Sturmbataillon was further raised when Jean Ollivier, 4th Company's old commander, was found alive and well and fighting with a neighbouring SS unit after partly recovering from his earlier wound. He rejoined his French comrades in the line.

The day did not pass so quietly for the detached 1st Company. The Company was split into its remaining platoons and positioned around the Belle-Alliance-Platz to halt incoming Soviet attacks. Fragmented and unsupported, the fate of the Company was sealed. The platoons fought in the smoke and choking dust all day, defending their brick barricades and even mounting local counter-attacks, but all were anxious to rejoin their comrades in the SS-Sturmbataillon for the coming finale of the battle. Eventually they were released by the Sector Commander and in the hours of darkness one of the 2nd Company's platoon commanders, de Lacaze, appeared at Fenet's headquarters with the survivors. They were not many. Waffen-Oberjunker Croisille's platoon was not among the survivors; it had last been seen attacking a force of T-34s with panzerfäusts, and then had disappeared in the smoke and confusion. Both of Waffen-Hauptsturmführer Jean Croisille's two sons serving with the Charlemagne were now dead, the first in Galicia at Mokré, and the second here in Berlin. More than that, the Company Commander, 22-year-old Waffen-Untersturmführer Labourdette, was not there either. The third ever man to volunteer for the French Waffen-SS Labourdette had fought in Galicia, in the SS-Sturmbrigade, and Pomerania before coming to Berlin. He was shot and killed covering the withdrawal of his remaining men down the underground tunnels.

A day that had started well with Ollivier's return and the awards for bravery, had ended in tragedy. Two of the five original company commanders were gone, and half the men too. Saturday would bring more death to the Frenchmen.

Tank busting at Belle-Alliance-Platz

On the morning of Saturday 28 April the Nordland defensive line came under increasing pressure from Soviet tank and infantry attacks around the Belle-Alliance-Platz, as the Russians stormed across the Landwehr Canal towards the Chancellery and Hitler himself. In their new role as designated 'tank busters' the French SS grenadiers first formed one commando under SS-Oberstumführer von Wallenrodt, and then a second under the 38-year-old Waffen-Oberscharführer Lucien Hennecart. Soon all of Charlemagne, including Weber's Kampfschule, were committed to the battle round the Platz.

The French *modus operandi* for tank busting was simple. Firstly if there were any accompanying Russian infantry they would either be killed or pinned down by machine gun fire. Then the panzerfäust men would work their way through the rubble to within a short distance from the now unsupported tanks, and then blow them to pieces. Attack after attack was broken up in this way with Russian casualties mounting. Between assaults the Soviets pounded the area with heavy and sustained artillery fire. This collapsed roofs, floors and even whole buildings, and as always under such bombardment, the defenders suffered terrible casualties, but also were able to use the resultant ruins to their advantage. It was during this day's fighting that the men from Charlemagne really began to establish their reputation as an elite in the defence of the city. Enemy fire whittled away at the unlucky and those less able, and those who were left were increasingly the lucky and the exceptional.

Having only been in the city for three days the remaining grenadiers were already experts at the savage fighting that is urban combat. Armed with nothing more sophisticated than assault rifles, grenades, knives and panzerfäusts they were taking on the might of the Red Army and holding them. They were not going to win, but they were going to resist. This then was the much talked about toughness and attitude, the so-called *Härte*, of the true combat soldier, Germany's famed *Frontschwein*.

Shells sent up a constant pall of brick dust, and mixed in with this was a curtain of black smoke from burning buildings and vehicles that almost blocked out the sun. No one could hear anything over the incessant noise from explosions and firing weaponry, not to mention the immense din from tank engines and tracks, and in the midst of all this small knots of French SS grenadiers kept up a withering fire at any advancing Russians. It was also now that they began to operate independently as only elite, experienced troops can do, and still be effective. For instance, Roger Roberto's section of runners set light to a multi-storey building from the cellars to smoke out the Russian infantrymen hiding inside. Over fifty came running out and were shot dead by Roberto and his men as they tried to escape the smoke and flames. Roberto himself then went to clear enemy snipers from the rooftops, and after killing a good many was blinded by grenade shrapnel. His comrade Maxime de Lacaze, now 1st Company's Commander, was hit by a sniper that Roberto didn't get, and evacuated, badly wounded but alive.

Shrapnel was definitely the biggest danger to the Frenchmen, and the majority of their casualties were caused by razor sharp, hot fragments of metal from artillery, tank, mortar and anti-tank gun rounds. Waffen-Unterscharführer Jean-Louis Puechlong was one such casualty; he and a band of comrades were hit by an anti-tank gun shell and he lost a leg as a result. To be killed or wounded by small arms fire, like de Lacaze, was relatively rare. Saturday drew to a close with the SS men still in control of the roads leading from the Belle-Alliance-Platz, despite the best efforts of the Red Army to take it.

Defence at Puttkamer Strasse

Sunday 29 April dawned, and with it came the realisation to Fenet that he would have to withdraw the remains of his Battalion if they were to carry on the fight. The French front line was now nothing more than a series of heaps of rubble surrounded by dead and dying men from both sides, and interspersed with burning tank hulks. However Fenet hesitated, the Chancellery was only a few hundred metres away as it was, and every step back taken by the Frenchmen brought the Soviets closer to their goal and the end of the battle.

While Fenet thought through his options his men continued to fight like demons. Tank busting was now regarded as some sort of lethal competition! Leading the scores were Waffen-Unterscharführers Eugène Vaulot and Roger Albert-Brunet, both of the Kampfschule, on four and three tanks respectively. It was Albert-Brunet's fate to be murdered after surrendering by a Russian soldier screaming "SS, SS!"

But it was absolutely clear to all that bravery would not suffice for long; the SS-Sturmbataillon Charlemagne had to fall back. Still the Russians came on. They now resorted to advancing rows of tanks almost wedged together by their tracks to stop the dreaded panzerfäust teams infiltrating between them and picking them off one by one. This tactic simply did not work in the confined space of rubble strewn streets, and yet more Soviet tanks were turned into burning scrap as a result. The frustrated Russians now began to use their awesome firepower in earnest against the stubborn defenders. Any building from which the French SS men fired was systematically blown to bits by concentrated direct fire from the Soviets. Groups of T-34s, self-propelled guns, and anti-tank guns would focus all their fire on a single building at a time until there was nothing left. If the French grenadiers didn't get out in time they were buried in the rubble.

All contact had been lost with any flanking units; they had either withdrawn or been wiped out, and Fenet and his men were all alone. He now made the decision he had delayed almost all day, and gave orders to withdraw to a new line based on Puttkamer Strasse, some fifty or so metres to the rear. Through the smoke and flames the orders for withdrawal went out via the runners to the scattered fighting sections, and in some kind of order they melted back to the new line and started to dig in again. Fenet and his Headquarters staff were some of the last to fall back, and they left the Russians to continue their building-by-building demolition of the old defensive position. The fight was not yet over for the French SS!

However, it was over for Jean Ollivier, the previously wounded and evacuated Commander of the 4th Company. Caught in an artillery barrage he was badly wounded and evacuated again, this time for good. He would fight no more.

The pullback was successful, but did not bring the Charlemagne anything other than temporary relief. The Soviets advanced again and hit the new line with the usual howls of artillery and tank rounds, and the French reply was the same, the automatic fire of MG42s and *Sturmgewehrs* interspersed with the guttural coughs of repeated panzerfäust strikes. How the French grenadiers kept fighting was nothing short of miraculous. The Soviets had an inexhaustible supply of men, machines and ammunition, and continually fed in new units when the old ones were shattered. The French had no such luxuries, and now even the ammunition they so desperately needed began to run out. The panzerfäusts in particular were almost all gone, and without them the Charlemagne would be overrun in minutes. Fresh stocks were fetched from the caches at the Chancellery a few hundred metres away, but the supply was not enough and the journey extremely hazardous. Without ammunition the defence was over.

The SS-Sturmbataillon Charlemagne was now fighting for its life. The Russians gave them no let up, and attack was followed by attack, with seemingly endless Soviet tanks and infantrymen throwing themselves onto the French guns. The slaughter was dreadful. Most of the grenadiers had now not slept for over forty-eight hours, and only eaten what they could scavenge; even water was in short supply. The Russians, meanwhile, were growing increasingly exasperated at the tenacity of the few defenders. Their goal was in sight and in two days' time it was one of the highlights of the communist calendar, May Day, the Workers' Day, and they were determined that the Chancellery would fall on such an auspicious anniversary. The Soviets pushed forward through the night, using flamethrowers to try to winkle the defenders out; those caught in its fiery embrace had the air in their lungs burnt up even as their skin blistered, their hair caught fire and their internal organs began to be cooked. It was a manner of death that all rightly feared. Any Soviet infantry seen carrying the bulky fuel tanks or nozzles of the dreaded weapons were priority targets and shot on sight.

François Appolot and Eugène Vaulot

Acts of bravery were commonplace amongst the French SS grenadiers during the defence of Berlin. As in all battles most went unnoticed and unremembered, except by those directly involved. However, the exploits of two men were of such a calibre that they were recognised by the award of Nazi Germany's highest decoration, the Knight's Cross. Worn round the neck it was the most coveted of medals. In German military parlance at the time, to win one was to 'cure your throat ache'. Winning the medal was seen as the ultimate accolade and a unit's tally of such medals was a gauge of its fighting quality. An analysis of Waffen-SS men who won the Knight's Cross reveals that the classic Waffen-SS units like the Leibstandarte, Das Reich, Totenkopf and Wiking received the most. These four divisions alone received 55% of all Knight's Crosses awarded to the nominal thirty-eight divisions of the Waffen-SS. A further eight divisions, all of which were German, West European or Scandinavian, won another 29% of the total, so that less than a third of Waffen-SS formations earned nearly 90% of all Knight's Crosses.

Up until the battle in Berlin no one in Charlemagne had won a Knight's Cross. The defence of Belle-Alliance-Platz and Puttkamer Strasse was to change all that. François Appolot served as a senior sergeant in the 28e regiment d'infanterie de forteresse, the fortress infantry, during the German invasion of 1940. Like so many of his comrades he was taken captive on the capitulation and then became a worker in Germany. He was working up on the Baltic coast in Königsberg in 1944 when he was caught *in flagrante* with the wife of his German boss. Given the choice of either being sent to a concentration camp or joining the Wehrmacht, Appolot went for the Kriegsmarine. He ended up in one of the units destined for amalgamation into the French Waffen-SS. After undergoing training in Sennheim until the end of June 1944, Appolot then became a platoon commander with the rank of Waffen-Oberscharführer in the SS-Sturmbrigade Frankreich. He served with distinction in Pomerania in the Compagnie d'Honneur, survived the fighting at Elsenau, and on return became a section commander in Weber's new Kampfschule. In this role he went with his men to Berlin and ended up, panzerfäust in hand, fighting around the Belle-Alliance-Platz.

In many ways it had been a series of accidents that had put François Appolot in the path of the Soviet advance, but his exploits were no accident. Again and again, through a withering blizzard of Red Army shelling, he would grab a panzerfäust tube and work his way forward to where the metal monsters were. By 29 April Appolot had destroyed the remarkable personal tally of six tanks. He was then awarded the Knight's Cross. Most believed that he was then killed in the final days of the defence of Berlin, but in reality he survived. Remarkably he got out of the burning city by joining a group of French labourers trying to get home and then on crossing the border into France he proceded to drop out of sight. Passing himself off as one of the many hundreds of thousands of refugees returning home after the war he settled quietly in eastern France, married and raised a family, without anyone knowing of his past. However, many years later his son read a book on the activities of the Charlemagne Division, and recognised his father from the description given. Finally the secret was out, and the Appolot family came to terms with what had happened so long ago in the fire and blood of the war.

Eugène Vaulot was a 21-year-old Parisian, who had left his job as a tradesman to join the LVF in 1941. He had fought as a legionnaire in Russia, been promoted and won the Iron Cross 2nd Class for bravery before being wounded in action and invalided out of the service in 1943. Unable to settle back into civilian life in France, he joined the Kriegsmarine and completely by chance ended up in the same unit as François Appolot. Just like Appolot, he then transferred across to the SS-Sturmbrigade Frankreich and served with distinction in Pomerania at Elsenau, this time winning the Iron Cross 1st Class in combat. Again like Appolot, he was then made a section commander in the Kampfschule, but only at the rank of Waffen-Unterscharführer. In Berlin, along with his friend Roger Albert-Brunet, he became a tank killer par excellence, turning the nerve wracking action of stalking and blowing up Soviet tanks almost into a game. By the end of 29 April his personal tally was a truly awesome eight tanks. He was awarded his Knight's Cross in the Divisional Headquarters tramcar by Krukenberg himself. Eugène Vaulot, winner of the Knight's Cross, Iron Cross 1st and 2nd Class, veteran of three years of combat on the Russian Front, finally ran out of luck on 2 May 1945, when he was shot and killed by a Red Army sniper.

A new week dawns

Monday 30 April came with no respite for the ever dwindling band of French defenders. Fenet moved his Headquarters again to a nearby library cellar, and this building quickly became the centre of resistance for the few stubborn SS men left alive and fighting. Only the most seriously wounded were evacuated now; the most a man could hope for in most cases was a paper bandage from a medic, maybe a couple of hours' rest, and then it was back into the line to carry on the fight. Only the very toughest were left now. These were the men with no give in them, no compromise, and the Russians were paying the price. By the end of that day there were twenty-one burning Soviet tank hulks around the library, the victims of the ever present panzerfäusts and SS grenadiers who knew how to use them.

Soviet armour and infantry were loath to carry on the assault; they knew how close it was to the end and had no wish to die now. Despite everything that was thrown at them the library was still, unbelievably, in French hands at the end of that long, dreadful day.

Unbeknown to the French SS grenadiers at the library slugging it out with waves of Soviet tanks and infantry, a few hundred metres away, deep in the safe earth of the Führer Bunker in the Chancellery Gardens, a last drama was being played out. Nazi Germany's Chancellor, Head of State, Supreme Commander of the Armed Forces and head of the Nazi Party was marrying his long time mistress, Eva Braun. Following the simple civil ceremony the now-married couple retired to a room for privacy, whereupon Eva Hitler took poison and Adolf Hitler blew his own brains out.

It was all over. The Nazi 'dream' was finally dead, and the world could now breathe again, but no one in the outside world knew it yet. Back at the library the fighting went on.

The news spreads

May Day arrived. The world had now shrunk for Fenet and his remaining SS grenadiers. There were fewer than fifty men still capable of resistance, and their world on Tuesday 1 May 1945 was now a patch of Berlin a few hundred metres square. They moved position yet again to the Sicherheitshauptamt, the Ministry of Security, near the infamous old Gestapo Headquarters and torture cellars on Prinz-Albrecht Strasse. They fought like robots now, unthinking and unfeeling. Not a round or a panzerfäust was wasted, the Russians were still falling in droves to the tiny band of Frenchmen, but everywhere else in the capital resistance was finally collapsing.

The Russians knew it was the end and could stand off a few hundred metres from the beleaguered French defenders and organise their assaults in plain sight, as the grenadiers had no weapons left with either a substantial range or real hitting power to hurt the confident Russians. The massed Soviet armour would then stay static and pour high explosive rounds into every building in sight, supported by ranks of artillery pieces firing over open sights. All the Charlemagne men could do was sit there and take it, and wait for the inevitable Soviet advance. When they were up close, their turn would finally come, and the Russians would pay in blood. But everyone knew this couldn't go on for long; the end was definitely in sight. Meanwhile around them everything was happening apace. General Krebs had left the Führer Bunker and was negotiating with the Soviets for a ceasefire. But the Red Army wasn't interested in talk of any ceasefire, it was unconditional surrender or nothing. Krukenberg was summoned to the Führer Bunker and told of Hitler's death by Brigadeführer Wilhelm Mohnke, a high ranking and well-known figure in the Waffen-SS and ex-member of the Leibstandarte Division. Mohnke was the most senior SS officer in the Bunker after Herman Fegelein was shot for desertion earlier in the battle. He asked Krukenberg if he would take over the command of the city's defence, but Krukenberg refused stating that any such defence was utterly pointless at this stage; the battle and the city were lost. Mohnke agreed. The Gauleiter of Berlin and his wife, Joseph and Magda Goebbels, proceeded to murder their six young children, five daughters and one son, with poison and then took cyanide themselves. The whole pack of cards was now coming down, and the SS grenadiers of Charlemagne were fast becoming an isolated and singular island of resistance, and that island was shrinking.

Another handful of French grenadiers were killed that day, including the émigré Russian and ex-LVF legionnaire 'Prince' Protopopoff, felled by shrapnel. His close friend, Pierre Rostaing, was now almost certainly the last legionnaire left standing. Rostaing had been wounded at least twice in the city's defence over the last few days, and had been given up for dead on more than one occasion, but his luck had held. However, his company was gone. In reality there hadn't been any company structures for two days now, there was no point and the men were past that. All that was left was the will to fight, and Fenet had directed them in that. It looked as if the end of Charlemagne had come, there would be no survivors, but fate had not yet finished with the French Waffen-SS. As his last order as Commandant of Berlin's defence, General Weidling gave permission for a breakout by anyone who was willing to chance it. Those determined to get out were to form themselves into small groups that night, and head to the north-west and try to get through the Russian lines. Fenet and his men now had a chance.

The breakout

Back at his Divisional Headquarters in the underground tramcar, Krukenberg called his last officers' briefing and gave his final set of orders of the war. He would lead the breakout personally, small rearguards would stay in place to cover the withdrawal, and the Division would begin to move out from 2300hrs that night. The entire operation was a disaster from the start. All attempts to find a route out through the Soviet troops drew enormous fire, and casualties were very heavy. Men who had fought like titans for days of desperate defence, keeping the Red Army at bay, were now butchered in their hundreds as they vainly tried to find an escape route. Most of the troops attempting to get out were soon split into myriads of small groups with no direction, few weapons and little ammunition. Group by group they were either wiped out or captured. Those who got out were very few and very lucky. Some Charlemagne men were included in the general breakout. Wilhelm Weber was wounded and then captured trying to lead a group out, and Eugène Vaulot, he of the recently awarded Knight's Cross, was killed trying to get through the Soviet lines.

Krukenberg was not one of the lucky few to escape. He was soon separated from his troops in the confusion, and after narrowly evading capture once, ended up finally surrendering to a Russian artilleryman. So went into captivity the last commander of 33rd Waffen-Grenadier-Division der SS Charlemagne (französische Nr.1). However, Fenet's Frenchmen were not with Krukenberg. The liaison officer sent to inform Fenet of the breakout, and give him his orders, didn't get through. So as the Norge and Danmark regiments quietly melted away from their positions to begin their escape, Fenet and the last few Charlemagne grenadiers stayed at their posts waiting for the next Soviet attack, the attack they were sure would be the last they would ever see. The wait was in vain.

The bitter end

An eerie silence now descended over Berlin, and for the French SS grenadiers used to the crashing crescendo of close quarter combat, it was completely unnerving. Small patrols were sent out to the flanks, in the early hours of the morning of 2 May, to make contact with other defenders. They returned and all reported the same thing: there was no-one there, the Charlemagne was alone! Confused but wary, Fenet took the survivors back to the Air Ministry building and there found a scene of complete capitulation. A Luftwaffe officer told Fenet of Hitler's suicide and Krebs' negotiations, and said that surrender was imminent. There were Russian soldiers mingling unmolested with the remaining Germans and swapping cigarettes. Everywhere there were smiles and waves, for Fenet and his men the scene was surreal. The SS men were at a loss, they had suffered so much in the last eight days, lost so many comrades, only now to find it was seemingly over. Confirmation was needed, they had not seen the Chancellery fall, if there was any resistance left it would be there, so that was where they would go.

Still armed to the teeth with small arms, panzerfäusts and as much ammunition as they could carry, Fenet and his men made their way cautiously through the city ruins towards the Chancellery. They passed Krukenberg's old Headquarters in the Stadtmitte U-Bahn, now completely deserted, and then went to Kaiserhof U-Bahn station opposite the Chancellery. The sight that met their eyes was of a sea of Soviet tanks flying red banners, and drunken Red Army soldiers looting everything in sight. It really was over. Dispirited and demoralised the Frenchmen decided to try to use the underground tunnels to escape out to Potsdam, where they had heard there were still German troops fighting. Ever so carefully the last few dozen French SS men made their way through the tunnels, sometimes having to dig through collapsed sections, but always moving west. At Potsdamer Platz the underground suddenly went 'over ground'. It was midday and there was no way they could chance that section in the light, they would have to hole up and wait for dark.

Dispersing into tiny groups of comrades they hid themselves in the nooks and crannies of the tunnels. Fenet and four others hid behind a wall of wicker baskets, where they were soon joined by Roger Albert-Brunet. However luck was not with them, and Soviet troops soon began to search the area. One by one they found the knots of grenadiers. Fenet's group was uncovered late in the afternoon, and Rostaing's party actually went undiscovered until midnight. But in the end almost every survivor of Charlemagne went into the bag. It was an ignominious end to an epic struggle. The outcome had never been in doubt, but the SS grenadiers of Charlemagne had fought with distinction and heroism; testament to that were the burning carcasses of almost 100 Russian armoured vehicles and huge numbers of brown smocked infantrymen who had fallen to their last stand.

Names to remember

Henri Fenet ended the war as Charlemagne's last field commander, and led it during its finest hour, the defence of Berlin. Wounded, but undaunted, he demonstrated courage and leadership throughout the whole mammoth struggle from the counter-attack at Neukölln, through tank busting at Belle-Alliance-Platz, and the final savagery of Puttkamer Strasse and the library. His SS-Sturmbataillon Charlemagne had started with a strength of around 300 men, and by the end Fenet was leading at most thirty men. Henri Joseph Fenet joined Appolot and Vaulot as a recipient of the Knight's Cross for bravery during the defence of the Reich capital.

Pierre Rostaing went into the battle as a senior NCO Company Commander and the flag waver for the old LVF. He had fought the Red Army since the Winter War in Finland in 1939–40, and was now there at the end, just yards from the shattered Reich Chancellery. To the end Rostaing was the epitome of the professional soldier; he had survived countless close shaves and ended the war as one of the most decorated foreign volunteers to serve with the German armed forces during World War II.

André Bayle spent the Battle for Berlin with his comrades in Stalin's gulag system. In many ways his struggle for survival was just as tough as the one endured by those who fought in the ruins of Berlin.

CHAPTER XI

Aftermath: The Reckoning

World War II saw the greatest ever number of human war casualties in recorded history. Whole generations from the fighting nations were almost wiped out, alongside the deliberate and planned near destruction of the entire Jewish race in the Holocaust. Across Europe and the Soviet Union the destruction was unprecedented. All wars are calamities, but the sheer scale of the brutality and horror of World War II gives it an unenviable position in world history. In Yugoslavia for example one in ten of the entire population, 1.7 million human beings, died. This was in a country that was conquered by the Germans in less than a month, but where the resistance, collaboration and subsequent bitter civil war raged until the dawn of 1945. Retribution by the victors always follows on from the end of wars, and it was therefore almost inevitable that after such a cataclysmic event as this war the bill of reckoning was going to be extraordinarily high. The end of the war in Europe also brought revelations about the true nature of Nazism, with the discovery of the concentration camps of Auschwitz-Birkenau, Treblinka, Buchenwald and the rest of the industrial machinery of mass human extermination. As the guns at last fell silent, people all over the continent had time to assess the staggering cost of the conflict forced on them by Hitler and his minions. In such an atmosphere mercy was a scarce commodity, and those foreigners who had fought alongside the Germans, for whatever reasons, found themselves very much on the losing end.

Revenge in east and west

The end of the war saw some of the largest mass movements of people in history as immense numbers of people underwent huge migrations, some voluntary and others forced. Nazi Germany had brought millions of foreign labourers to the Reich for its factories and farms to keep its war machine going, and those who had survived were desperate to get home. There were also huge numbers of prisoners-of-war from all sides festering in camps, and now longing for repatriation. For so many it was a vain hope. Whilst the Western Allies were incredibly keen to get their servicemen back, the same was not true of the Soviet Union. Stalin was paranoid about the exposure of his soldiers and civilians to what he saw as the corrupting influence of the West. So for tens of thousands of men and women who had survived the brutality and maltreatment of Hitler's Germany their welcome home was to their own land's notorious gulag system.

There were also significant numbers of people from across the Soviet Union, and Tito's now-communist Yugoslavia, who had sided with the Germans, most of them to fight the communist yoke. For these people their journey home was to end in death. For the freedom loving Cossacks, Vlasov's anti-communist Russians, nationalist Ukrainians, fascist Croats, royalist Serbs and nationalist Balts they knew that a long sentence in a gulag was the best they could hope for, a bullet in the head being far more likely and the end result for so many. Stalin was determined to exact the full measure of victor's justice from Germany, and for the huge numbers of German POWs in Soviet hands, surviving immediate capture was only a reprieve. They then spent many years in camps all over the Soviet Union, often being used as slave labour to rebuild the country after all the destruction it had suffered. Stalingrad in particular was rebuilt using German prisoners. Conditions for the POWs in the camps were universally appalling; well over 2,000,000 Axis (German, Italian, Hungarian, Rumanian, and all the volunteer nationalities) POWs died in labour and punishment camps in the Soviet Union and Balkans both during and after the war. For example, of the 90,000 German soldiers from the doomed 6th Army who surrendered at Stalingrad, only some 5,000 ever returned to Germany alive years after the end of the war. The last prisoners were not released by the Soviet Union until well into the 1950s. However, to put this brutality in context it must be remembered that this was still less than the number of Red Army prisoners who died in German captivity from execution, torture and appalling mistreatment. Atrocity breeds atrocity.

Even in this general orgy of vengeance the Waffen-SS were seen as a special case by the victors, and many men who surrendered wearing the *sig* runes didn't even get to a camp due to the reputation they had among their conquerors. Twenty prisoners from the 12th SS Panzer Division Hitlerjugend were allegedly shot by British forces at Soltau. At Oberpframmen eight SS men were executed, at Lippach thirty-six, at Eberstetten seventeen, at Utting six, at Haar another six, and at Webling fifty-three SS men were shot after surrendering. In no way can these atrocities be excused, but the perpetrators of the massacres at Le Paradis, Malmédy and Taganrog could surely expect little mercy.

For the western Europeans who had sided with the Germans the outlook was somewhat brighter than for their comrades from the East, but they were still to suffer. Over 60,000 Dutch were stripped of their citizenship after being interned in special camps. Many Flemish volunteers who returned to Belgium were forced to walk through jeering crowds being constantly beaten, and approximately 200 were murdered by the baying mob. Danish ex-SS soldiers were denied any pension rights or government aid. Some of the worst retribution, however, fell on those who had never worn a uniform during the conflict. In the East the huge number of racial Germans, the Volksdeutsche, in now liberated Hungary, Rumania, Czechoslovakia, and of course the annexed areas of eastern Germany handed over to Poland, were now seen by their new governments as the 'enemy within'. After all, in the eyes of both the new administrations and the majority populace, many of their number had fought in the Waffen-SS Volksdeutsche divisions and were seen as traitors. Whole populations now suffered expulsion from their ancestral homes, with approximately 18 million ethnic Germans having to leave their lands and head west. It is estimated that some three million lost their lives in the forced expulsions. This was a truly terrible act of ethnic cleansing.

For the Frenchmen who had fought with the Germans it was their time to pay the price of losing. The most infamous incident occurred at Bad Reichenhall in the south of Germany. Thirteen members of the Charlemagne and LVF were captured by the Americans in Bavaria; some were recovering from wounds and some were trying to escape the final collapse. They were subsequently handed over to their Gaullist countrymen of the American-equipped 2nd Free French Armoured Division. On 8 May 1945, the day the European war officially ended, they were brought before the Division's commanding officer, the famed General Leclerc. The General asked the volunteers why they were wearing a German uniform. One of the volunteers shot back a reply asking the General why he was wearing an American one. It sealed the men's fate. A firing quad was hastily convened and the prisoners were taken to local farmland and shot on the spot. They included ex-LVF Lieutenant Paul Briffaunt, born in Hanoi, Vietnam in French Indochina; Briffaunt was wounded in Russia and demobilised thereafter. Waffen-Obersturmführer Serge Krotoff from Madagascar had served in Pomerania with the Charlemagne commanding the anti-tank guns that had so bravely held off the Soviet tank assaults at Elsenau until his battery was destroyed and he was wounded. Waffen-Untersturmführer Robert Duffas and SS-Schütze Raymond Payras from Sri Lanka also served with Charlemagne in Pomerania. These were the only victims to be formally identified, the rest are unknown. Only one of the captured prisoners survived, the son of an old friend of Leclerc, and as such separated from his comrades, reprieved and quietly sent home to his family.

The other Allied conquering nations also seemed to learn from the oppression that the Nazis practised. An American Army occupation proclamation announced that if any GI was killed by a German, twenty-five hostages would be shot in reprisal. Not to be outdone, a proclamation by the French in their sector of occupation announced that no fewer than fifty hostages would be shot if a French soldier was killed.

France: the unforgiven

France has had immense difficulty coming to terms with the events and significance of World War II for French society. There was the trauma of the military and political collapse in just five weeks in 1940, followed by four years of Nazi occupation. There was the emergence of the collaborationist Vichy regime and with it the shameful complicity in the deportation of over 76,000 French Jews for extermination in *'la grande rafle'* of 1942. These were events and acts that would rip any nation asunder. Added to this was the virtual civil war that had been fought between the extreme Right and Left, between the collaborators and the resistors, and it is easy to see why it has been extraordinarily hard for France to fully face its past.

There were some 600,000 French war deaths in World War II, but the nature of those deaths was far more complex than the one-and-a-half million dead of its predecessor conflict World War I. Some 200,000 of the total died in military action (90,000 in 1939–40 alone). The Vichy regime was responsible for another 135,000 killed (including the 76,000 French Jews of whom only some 2,000 returned alive). The Resistance, both Gaullist and communist, was responsible for at least 10,000 French deaths both during and after the occupation, and a further 7,000 collaborators were sentenced to death after the war by the French authorities; however, only 767 were actually executed. The widespread settling of old scores after the occupation was called *'l'épuration'*, with summary executions and punishments occurring all over France. Perhaps most common was the practice of the shaving of the heads of women deemed to have been too 'friendly' with the Germans. This topic, female fraternisation, and its inevitable biological aftermath, has left a permanent scar on French society.

France's 'Boche babies' cry out

In supposedly 'Aryan' countries such as Norway and Denmark, official Nazi blessing was given to German servicemen fathering children with local girls. In Himmler's mind this could only strengthen and expand the gene pool of the 'master race', but such activity was not viewed in the same benevolent light in 'non-Aryan' lands. This included the French-speaking Walloons of Belgium and of course France itself, where sexual relationships with *'les petites françaises'* were banned. However, as every army knows, trying to keep soldiers away from local girls is akin to trying to build a ladder to reach the Moon. The children born to such illicit unions have suffered terrible abuse through no fault of their own, but rather because of a shared sense of national guilt. The recent book, *Enfants maudits* (*Blighted Children*), by Jean-Paul Picaper and Ludwig Norz, estimated that about 200,000 'French' children were fathered by German soldiers during the four years of occupation. Liberated France not only punished the women who had consorted with the enemy, but also inflicted lifetime punishment on their illegitimate children, the so-called 'Boche bastards'.

Daniel Roux, born in 1943 in Brittany of his mother's affair with a Wehrmacht officer, described how his grandmother kept him locked up every night in a hen coop behind the house after the war ended, while a local council official told all the villagers at a public meeting in the church that they had a 'baby Boche' in their midst. Even now discussion of this topic is *verboten* in French society and political life. Picaper and Norz had enormous trouble even finding a publisher who was willing to take the book on. It must be remembered that those illegitimate children and their descendants now number about a million people in France. These same children suffered further from rejection, not only by their French side but also by the Germans. German families often stigmatised the children, believing still that the French were an inferior race; this was not the same for the offspring of affairs with the Scandinavians and the Dutch and Flemish, who were looked after as 'Aryans'.

Secret army?

Latecomers to the cause of the French Resistance often covered up their own earlier inactivity in the war in a welter of accusation and counter-accusation when liberation finally came. Those Frenchmen and women who had resisted so bravely since before D-Day were also keen to see retribution against those who had hunted them during the occupation. But after an initial bout of bloodletting, France wanted to forget. It wanted to remember the slaughter in Oradour-sur-Glane, not the shame of the Jewish round-up at the Vélodrome d'Hiver; it wanted to remember Buchenwald (the destination camp for political prisoners and resisters), and not Auschwitz (home of the Birkenau extermination camp and the destination for French Jews).

Recent trials have refreshed memories; in 1987 Klaus Barbie the 'Butcher of Lyons', murderous head of the Gestapo in the city during the war, and the man credited with torturing the Resistance hero, Jean Moulin, to death after he was supposedly betrayed by a fellow Frenchmen, led to a re-examination of active French participation in Nazi oppression. Vichy luminaries have also been finally brought to trial: Paul Touvier in 1994, and Maurice Papon in 1997–8, casting light on a dark period of French history.

But for many Vichy officials it was an all too easy transition to the new government post-Liberation, and questions about their wartime records were usually buried. France's efforts to come to terms with this legacy have been patchy and half-hearted, even when questions could be asked of the most powerful in the land. The Socialist French President of the 1980s, François Mitterand himself, was a wartime Vichy official whose record and conversion to the Resistance is still shrouded in mystery.

The end of Darnard

As for that figurehead of hate in Vichy, Joseph Darnard, he was virtually unemployed after the establishment of Charlemagne. With the Milice gone his power base had been stripped from him and he flailed around trying to re-establish some measure of authority in a world that no longer cared for him. But whatever Darnard was he was no coward, and unlike so many adherents and fellow travellers of the Third Reich he made no attempt to slink away to South America with looted diamonds in his pockets leaving his fellow countrymen to their fate. He was eventually captured by the Allies in the Nazi collapse of 1945 in Italy, and was handed over to the new French government for trial and retribution. Darnard's fate was never in doubt and a short imprisonment was followed by a trial and the inevitable guilty verdict. Joseph Darnard, 48 years old, and decorated eight times by his country for bravery in two World Wars, was executed by firing squad in Paris on 10 October 1945.

More revelations

Partly due to France's lack of willingness to face its past in an honest and contrite manner, there has been a continuing and steady stream of stories that occasionally prick the French national conscience. As a reflection of both the age of those involved, and of the changing face of political priorities, the stories that now come back to haunt France are often raised by the vexed question of pension rights. The following is a Reuters report from Paris of 18 March 1998:

> Nazi hunters said on Wednesday they had asked France to check lists of French people receiving German war pensions to see if there were any Nazi war criminals whom Bonn wanted to strike off their pensioners' roll.
> Rabbi Abraham Cooper of the Los Angeles-based Simon Wiesenthal Centre made the request to Jean-Maurice Ripert, diplomatic advisor to PM Lionel Jospin. 'There are 761 people in France who receive such pensions. Mr Rippert said the French Government would look

at the list and cooperate', Cooper told Reuters. German Labour Minister Norber Bluem said earlier in the month he would ask the Centre to help cross-check 33,137 pensions Germany pays abroad.

It is presumed most Frenchmen drawing pensions are from Alsace-Lorraine and were conscripted; about 130,000 Alsatians were conscripted and at least 40,000 were killed in the war. But French Veterans Affairs Ministry officials said they didn't believe any of the 761 were from Alsace-Lorraine. Germany compensated them under a lump sum scheme and they got French Government pensions. The same official said he believed the 761 were veterans of the LVF or the Charlemagne Division. Cooper also believes Charlemagne veterans might be included. The 8,000-man French SS division was composed of fanatical Nazi-sympathisers who were among the last defenders of Adolf Hitler's bunker as Russian forces conquered Berlin in 1945. Those who survived were jailed in France after the war while several of their officers were executed. Many Charlemagne troops were drawn from the hated Milice Française (French Militia) which hunted Resistance fighters and Jews. Cooper said they could be struck from the German pension rolls on the grounds the Milice 'violated the norms of humanity'.

Names to remember

Henri Joseph Fenet survived the war, badly wounded in the foot, but alive. Initially imprisoned in a Soviet POW camp, he was sent to a hospital north of Berlin for treatment. Once the wound was treated he was sent back to the POW camp, but it had been evacuated in the meantime. In one of those twists of fate that occur in the confusion of sudden peace the Russians then gave him a set of civilian clothes and told him he was free and that he should make himself scarce! This he did as fast as he could, joining a group of returning French labourers *en route* home. He tried to slip into France at Valenciennes, but was stopped and questioned. Although the blood group tattooing of all members of the SS was not common knowledge at that time, unfortunately for Fenet his interrogators did know and found his telltale tattoo. He was arrested, tried, convicted and sentenced to twenty years hard labour.

Following the passing of the *loi d'amnistie* of 1947, the French amnesty law, those serving prison sentences started to be quietly released, and Fenet was finally set free at the end of 1949. As a high profile survivor of the Charlemagne, he became a leading light in the veterans' organisation when it was set up after the war. Unlike many veterans, Fenet felt no need to emigrate to South America, or anywhere else for that matter, and stayed in his beloved France. He remained vocal about his political views and wartime experiences, even appearing in a range of television programmes and documentaries, in which he sought to faithfully represent his comrades, both alive and fallen. He attended many gatherings of former Waffen-SS men, where his status as a leading foreign volunteer and Knight's Cross holder always assured him a warm reception from his former comrades-in-arms. Henri Joseph Fenet died on 14 September 2002 in his Paris apartment. He was 83 years old.

Pierre Rostaing also survived Berlin and its aftermath. He wrote a book about his experiences in the war and was active in veterans' affairs for his old comrades from Charlemagne, attending many events and annual gatherings. He died in 1999.

André Bayle, still only 18 years old when the war ended, was finally repatriated to France from captivity in Soviet Russia. He was tried in a French court at Valenciennes for his wartime record. He went on to serve in the French Army as a paratrooper, before finally putting away his uniform, when he then became an author and advocate of his political views. He wrote two excellent books on his wartime service in Charlemagne and subsequent imprisonment and continues to be active and vocal in European-wide political affairs. He lives in the south of France.

Other veterans

What of other survivors of Charlemagne, what did the post-war world hold for them? Waffen-Hauptsturmführer Jean Bassompierre, the commander of II/RM captured by the Soviets after Körlin, managed to escape his captors and headed back to France. On realising France was too hot for him to stay he went to Italy *en route* to South America. Arrested as he boarded a South American bound ship in Naples, he was extradited back to France and tried for his service with the Milice. Convicted, he was shot by a firing squad from his old regiment, the Chasseurs Alpins, on 20 April 1948.

Waffen-Standartenoberjunker Maxime de Lacaze, platoon commander from the SS-Sturmbattaillon Charlemagne's 1st Company in Berlin, was captured in a Berlin dressing station receiving medical treatment. He escaped only to be wounded again, mistaken for a foreign forced labourer, and repatriated to France. Following his recovery back home, he followed the same escape route as Bassompierre to Italy, but was luckier and escaped to safety in South America.

Waffen-Sturmbannführer Jean de Vaugelas was another South America émigré after the war. He established a successful wine making and exporting business in Argentina, only to die in a suspicious car crash in 1957. In all probability he was murdered by French security service agents. His partner in the Argentinian business was none other than his fellow comrade-in-arms, René Fayard. Waffen-Untersturmführer Fayard, late commander of Charlemagne's anti-aircraft company in Pomerania, escaped one attempt on his life before before being shot in the head during a game of bridge in 1960. Almost certainly he was also murdered by the French security services. Gustav Krukenberg was sentenced to twenty-five years hard labour by a Soviet military tribunal, and ended up serving eleven years before being released. He stayed loyal to 'his Frenchmen' and was always welcome at reunions. He died in his hometown of Bonn on 23 October 1980.

Waffen-Untersturmführer Paul Pignard-Berthet was repatriated to France from Soviet captivity after being captured in the aftermath of Körlin. There he was tried for his wartime record in the Milice. Convicted, he was sentenced to five years hard labour. He was released in October 1948 after having served two years. Waffen-Sturmbannführer Emile Raybaud, having recovered from the wounds he received at Körlin in Pomerania, was also tried by a French court, and sentenced to death for his activities in the Milice. The sentence was commuted, and then he was released quietly after six years of imprisonment. He died in Provence on 7 September 1995.

For many survivors there were trials, convictions and sentences ranging from fines, to loss of civil rights, to terms of imprisonment. Although it should be noted that as the communist-led insurgency gathered pace in French Indochina, a number of ex-Charlemagne veterans were offered the chance to redeem themselves, according to the state, by volunteering for a specialist anti-insurgency unit fighting over there. Some did and others refused, but it is a fact that there were numbers of ex-LVF and Charlemagne men serving, often for many years, in the French armed forces after 1945 in imperial conflicts such as Indochina and Algeria.

CHAPTER XII

Military Impact. Was it worth it?

The question that forms the title of this chapter is one that has resonated unanswered since the end of the Second World War. Firstly, was the effort and resources dedicated to the employment of French volunteers in the German armed forces worth it in military terms, and secondly, was their designation as a Waffen-SS formation the best way to utilise them, again in military terms?

The military value of the Waffen-SS as a whole is a hugely controversial subject. No less a figure than Field Marshal Erich von Manstein wrote of the Waffen-SS in his memoirs:

> ...bravely as the Waffen-SS divisions always fought, and fine though their achievements may have been, there is not the least doubt that it was an inexcusable mistake to set them up as a separate military organisation. Hand-picked replacements which could have filled the posts of NCOs in the Army were expended on a quite inadmissible scale in the Waffen-SS, which in general paid a toll of blood incommensurate with its actual gains. Naturally this cannot be laid at the door of the SS troops themselves. The blame for such unnecessary consumption of manpower must lie with the men who set up these special units for purely political motives, in the face of opposition from all the competent Army authorities.
>
> In no circumstances must it be forgotten, however, that the Waffen-SS, like the good comrades they were, fought shoulder to shoulder with the Army at the Front and always showed themselves courageous and reliable. Without doubt a large proportion of them would have been only too glad to be withdrawn from the jurisdiction of a man like Himmler and incorporated into the Army.

This then was the considered view of one of Germany's greatest wartime commanders, the architect of the victory at Sedan and the taking of Sevastopol. But is such a judgement sound?

Was the Waffen-SS a more formidable force than the Wehrmacht that it fought alongside? It is certainly true that there were only a handful of Heer divisions, such as Panzer Lehr and the Grossdeutschland, who could boast a combat record that equalled or surpassed SS Leibstandarte or Das Reich. Why was this so? In terms of assessing military impact a great deal of subjectivity is inevitable in reaching a judgement. Manstein's view has obvious validity, particularly with regard to ordinary Waffen-SS soldiers being NCO material that the Army could have used to great advantage, but it is flawed in several major respects.

War as ideology

Firstly it takes no account of the ideological basis of the entire conflict. This was not a war fought for control of trade routes or even possession of territory. This was a return to the religious wars that raged across Europe after the Reformation. What was at stake in World War II were ideas, entire governmental systems and racial extinction. The winner's political system and ideology would dominate; the losers would be extinguished.

This can be difficult to grasp today as the political landscape has changed so dramatically, but for much of the 20th century the world was in one of its periodic eras of ideologies. World politics and governmental structures were dominated by competing ideas that were, more often than not, diametrically and violently opposed. Western-style liberal democracies were in the minority and dictatorships were still in the ascendant, even controlling much of the industrialised world, including Germany, Italy, Spain, Soviet Russia and much of Eastern Europe. The battle for the supremacy of ideas was still very much in full flow and was felt keenly by Europe's peoples. In the atmosphere of the time large numbers of ordinary people felt they were intimately involved in these political questions and that they had the ability, and even a duty, to influence them.

The idea of a volunteer European army, as the Waffen-SS became, fighting on a supra-national basis for a political philosophy, seems out of place now, but just a handful of years before it was the political Left of Europe that had created just such a force with the formation of the International Brigades fighting against Franco in the Spanish Civil War. The fact that the International Brigades didn't become anything like the superlative military force that the Waffen-SS did was more a reflection of the inadequacies of the Spanish Republic, rather than of the motivation and calibre of the international volunteers themselves. This 'internationalisation' of a cause that both inspires some, while inspiring dread and revulsion in others, is a recurring theme in history, and can be compared to the politics of today with the rise of militant Islam, as personified by the al-Qaeda organisation. This too is a cause that does not stop at national boundaries, and has an awesome power to bind together young men in particular to a wholly destructive purpose. The cause transcends not only nationality, but also ethnicity, class, educational and family background. As ever more revelations appear in the media of the backgrounds of convicted Islamic terrorists, and it is only too clear that to write them off as the media stereotype of the psychopathic, sub-normal dregs of society, is to grossly misjudge the threat. The comparison to the Waffen-SS is perhaps most appropoiate here in the examination of the individuals involved. To write them all off as 'deviants' may make their motivations and actions easier to comprehend and may help us sleep soundly at night, but it is an entirely false premise.

In such a war, as one of such competing ideologies, those most dedicated to the cause tend to fight with the most tenacity; absence of such belief in the fight greatly impacts on the fighting capability of troops. For example, note the performance of the Italian Army during the war which was poor to say the least, one of the major problems being lack of belief among Italians in what they saw as Mussolini's war. When dedicated Italian fascists did enter the battle their performance was almost universally superior, to not only their less enthusiastic comrades, but also a great shock to their opponents used to the propaganda image of Italians being only too willing to surrender as soon as the shooting started. Testimonies from Eighth Army troops who fought Italian Blackshirt units bear this out.

Looking at the conflict as a whole, there was not one mass surrender by Waffen-SS troops until the end of hostilities, nor was there one instance of major collapse at the Front (Kampfgruppe Nord's earliest poor performance at Sala in 1941 where troops ran away after taking a beating, could not be construed as a major collapse in a military sense). It would have been understandable militarily if the Totenkopf at Demyansk, or the Wiking and Wallonien at Cherkassy had surrendered; they were in terrible condition faced with overwhelming enemy forces, and yet they did not give in, but hung on with amazing tenacity. This was a major achievement, in particular when it is remembered that the Waffen-SS divisions were constantly destroyed, rebuilt, destroyed and rebuilt again. Such attrition on a massive scale would doom most units to lose all combat effectiveness, but the Waffen-SS remained a military elite until the very end precisely because of the human material they had.

> The willingness of the members of the Waffen-SS to go on fighting when it was clear that the war was lost can only be a source of wonder to today's generation. However, their experiences in the East undoubtedly added to their resolve to protect their homeland for as long as possible and at whatever cost.

This was the considered view of Michael Reynolds CB, retired Major General in the British Army, and military historian writing in 1997.

Heer versus Waffen-SS

It has also been hypothesised that the elite Waffen-SS Panzer divisions fought so well partly due to the fact that they received better, and on occasion more, equipment than their Heer counterparts. It is true that the SS Panzer divisions were substantially larger than those from the Wehrmacht, especially towards the end of the war. By 1944 all Panzer divisions contained an armoured regiment of two panzer battalions. Army Panzer divisions also contained two infantry regiments of two battalions each, but SS divisions mustered six infantry battalions. The average Army Panzer division went into the Battle of Normandy, for example, with almost 15,000 men at full strength, while SS divisions had up to 20,000 troops. To what extent this extra fire and manpower accounted for the SS divisions' fighting prowess is open to debate. It was certainly not the case that SS units received better equipment than their Army counterparts. When the Leibstandarte received the new Panzer Mark IVs with 75mm guns in 1942, Panzer Lehr and Grossdeutschland received similar amounts of identical equipment. Also the Waffen-SS divisions that received the best equipment were a minority, perhaps seven panzer and panzer grenadier divisions from a force of thirty-eight formations. The rest of the Waffen-SS order of battle comprised three cavalry divisions, six mountain divisions and the remainder were simple infantry units of varying quality and size. Most never even reached full divisional status, ranging in strength from a battalion to a regiment. In reality less than 30% of SS divisions were equipped for modern mobile warfare, but it is the exploits of these 'elite' SS Panzer divisions that have generally formed the reputation for military excellence of the Waffen-SS as a whole. But that reputation was, and is, awesome, and is commonly held. This enabled the Waffen-SS to have a military impact out of all proportion to their actual numbers, the retaking of Kharkov in 1943 by Paul Hausser's 1st SS Panzer Corps being the most classic example where they almost turned the tide back in Hitler's favour.

Casualties were heavy, some 180,000 Waffen-SS men were killed during the war, 400,000 were wounded and a further 70,000 reported missing (presumed killed). By 1944–5 the average age of the SS trooper was 19, with junior officers averaging just 20. Life expectancy on the battlefront was down to a meagre two months. It was not uncommon for even Divisional Commanders to be in their early to mid 30s; Hugo Kraas, Otto Kumm, Wilhelm Mohnke and Kurt Panzer Meyer among others. However, that must be viewed again in context. The Waffen-SS divisions were almost always in the forefront of the action, fighting wherever the battle was fiercest, and this fire brigade role was acknowledged at the time. Such action, by its very nature, is casualty heavy. The Waffen-SS also fought, overwhelmingly so, on the Eastern Front where losses of men in the thousands in battle was commonplace. For example, the loss of the

British 1st Parachute Division at Arnhem was seen as a terrible price to pay in terms of casualties in Operation Market Garden, but during the opening weeks of Operation Bagration in summer 1944 on the Russian Front, over twenty-five German divisions were totally wiped from the map.

The best judges, though, of the military value of the Waffen-SS must be from the enemy they fought. What was their view? The Russian, Major General Artemko of the 27th Red Army Corps, when captured in 1941, stated to his interrogators that 'his men breathed a sigh of relief when the SS Wiking Division was withdrawn from the line and replaced by a regular army unit'.

But, impressive as their achievements undoubtedly were, the Waffen-SS never succeeded in altering the outcome of the major battles of the war such as Stalingrad, Kursk or Normandy, and therefore the war itself. Their successes were only ever at a local level.

Charlemagne and morale

But in the context of Charlemagne, the dogged defence of Berlin by a mere handful of soldiers stands out. This 'morale' component of battle is difficult to quantify, but of undoubted immense value. To give an example, in the summer of 1944 prior to D-Day the hitherto much depleted 2nd SS Panzer Division Das Reich was rebuilt with thousands of raw recruits from twelve different nationalities, a large number of whom were unenthusiastic Franco-German Alsatian conscripts. One of them, Sadi Schneid, recalled after the war that his company of the divisional reconnaissance battalion had been on a night exercise for the first time in their training area in southern France, and on returning to camp their senior NCO, SS-Hauptscharführer 'Hascha' Kurz, a veteran of the Russian Front, was relieved not one of the young conscripts had deserted, and he delivered the following speech:

> Boys, if the Americans land one day, they won't be throwing potatoes, and I'm going to need all of you. That's why I keep emphasising to you that I don't need dead heroes but live ones. Remember everything I've taught you in training. A fraction of a second's carelessness at the Front, and it'll do for you. Once again, I urge you – trust me. If you do what I do, you've got a chance of coming out of it. Always obey my finger and my eye, and you'll thank yourselves later. I'll guarantee to do everything I can to keep your skins in one piece. Can I count on you?
> 'JAWOHL HAUPTSCHARFÜHRER' we shouted in chorus from the bottom of our hearts. 'SIEG HEIL, SIEG HEIL, SIEG HEIL', one might have imagined us at Munich after an oration from Hitler himself.'[1]

The spirit of the Waffen-SS was what made it truly different from its counterparts, and what made it able to get the very best out of its men and turn them into something that was militarily formidable.

Charlemagne as a military decision

The creation and use of Charlemagne were German decisions, despite the actions of Doriot, Darnard et al. Actually taking a physical part was a decision made by every individual Frenchman involved, but the entire episode was only made possible because of a conscious German effort. So did the Germans get what they wanted from Charlemagne? The short answer is of course 'No'. What they wanted was to win the war, and this they signally failed to do. The temptation here is to engage in 'what if' scenarios. The 'what if' industry, especially in military history, can and does fill entire library shelves with its output, capitalising on the fact that the human mind delights in exploring possibilities to a seemingly endless degree.

What if Hitler had not diverted the thrust of Barbarossa to the huge encirclement battles of the south, including Kiev, and instead had taken Moscow in 1941? What if the Nazis had enlisted the help and support of the Russian and Ukrainian peoples in a war of liberation from communism instead of treating them as Slavic sub-humans, would communism have been consigned to the dustbin of history and Hitler's Germany become a world superpower to rival the emergent United States? Thankfully we will never know, and it is also obvious that the success, or not, of Charlemagne does not rank with these hypotheses in the pantheon of the 'what if' industry. So perhaps the appropriate question to ask is 'could the effort and resource used by the Germans in creating and sustaining Charlemagne have been more effectively employed elsewhere?' This is a much more interesting question. In this context the value of Charlemagne can be seen in light of the many and varied comments made on the usefulness of the entire Waffen-SS. There is no doubt that as a military structure the Waffen-SS was an outstanding organisation. However, the military quality of that same organisation was incredibly inconsistent. It is impossible to place the fighting prowess of a unit like the Leibstandarte Adolf Hitler against the indescribable savagery of the thugs serving under Kaminski or Dirlewanger, or the almost total uselessness of the Handschar or Kama Divisions.

Charlemagne: recorded atrocities nil

One point that is of huge importance in reviewing the record of Charlemagne and the men who fought in it, is the fact that there are no recorded atrocities against its name. The subject of atrocities, massacres, brutality, executions, connection to the Holocaust, has stained the record of the entire Waffen-SS since the end of the fighting in Europe, and rightly so. In the heat of combat troops can and do commit acts which are both bloody and brutal, and must be condemned. This is the same for all sides; fighting for what is perceived as the 'right' side does not excuse murder. However, what was different for the Waffen-SS was not just its links to the other and more repellent arms of the SS organisation, such as the concentration camp guards and the dreaded extermination squads of the Einsatzgruppen, but the appearance to many on the outside that the committing of atrocities by its members was systematic and in some way officially condoned. Much is made by veterans and apologists for the Waffen-SS that, following their surrender at Arnhem, the British paratroopers who had held out so bravely against the SS troopers of the Frundsberg and Hohenstaufen Divisions were treated well as fellow warriors. But they miss the point that this standard of behaviour towards prisoners taken in combat is a basic rule of war, and it should not be the exception but the rule. When members of the Waffen-SS were taken prisoner, by the Western Allies at least, they expected to survive. Allied prisoners in the same situation feared the worst. This then was the legacy of all the undoubted bravery shown in battle, but forever tarnished by acts of brutality that must be remembered. Even elite divisions such as the Leibstandarte have the murders of over 100 American soldiers at Malmédy to their name, but for Charlemagne their record is unblemished. This is even more significant when you remember that all of the Division's actions were on the Russian Front which was a byword for brutality and excess.

The Charlemagne did indeed suffer from the classic problems associated with so many of the units raised in the final death throes of the Third Reich: lack of equipment, lack of combat experience, the chaos of impending defeat, overwhelming Soviet combat power and lack of experienced leadership. It had no 'winning time', such as other foreign formations like the Wiking, which had the time during the early years of German military dominance to participate in victories and learn its trade. This enabled these established formations to foster unit coherence and traditions, which later units such as Charlemagne sorely lacked; time was a luxury they did not have. It is in this light that Charlemagne's achievements must be viewed.

Note

1. Max Hastings, *Das Reich:The march of the 2nd SS Panzer Division through France 1944* (Pan, 1983).

Appendix: Waffen-SS Ranks

SS-Schütze	Private (this was the basic private rank; any speciality would be reflected in the title, e.g. Panzerschütze)
SS-Oberschütze	Senior Private (attained after six months' service)
SS-Sturmmann	Lance corporal
SS-Rottenführer	Corporal
SS-Unterscharführer	Lance Sergeant
SS-Junker	Officer candidate (substantive rank of SS-Unterscharführer)
SS-Scharführer	Sergeant
SS-Standartenjunker	Officer candidate (substantive rank of SS-Scharführer)
SS-Oberscharführer	Colour/staff Sergeant
SS-Hauptscharführer	Warrant Officer Class 2
SS-Standartenoberjunker	Officer candidate (substantive rank of SS-Hauptscharführer)
SS-Sturmscharführer	Warrant Officer Class 1 (after fifteen years' service)
SS-Untersturmführer	Second Lieutenant
SS-Obersturmführer	Lieutenant
SS-Hauptsturmführer	Captain
SS-Sturmbannführer	Major
SS-Obersturmbannführer	Lieutenant-Colonel
SS-Standartenführer	Colonel
SS-Oberführer	Brigadier equivalent
SS-Brigadeführer	Major-General
SS-Gruppenführer	Lieutenant-General
SS-Obergruppenführer	General
SS-Oberstgruppenführer	Colonel-General (only Sepp Dietrich ever attained this rank)

Bibliography

Ailsby, Christopher, *Hell on the Eastern Front: The Waffen-SS War in Russia 1941–1945*, Spellmount, 1998

Ailsby, Christopher, *Waffen-SS The Unpublished Photographs 1923–1945*, Bookmart, 2000

Bayle, André, *De Marseille à Novossibirsk*, Histoire et Tradition, 1992

Bayle, André, *San et Persante*, self-published, 1994

Beevor, Antony, *Berlin: The Downfall 1945*, Penguin, 2003

Bishop, Chris, *Hell on the Western Front: The Waffen-SS in Europe 1940–45*, Spellmount, 2003

Butler, Rupert, *SS-Wiking*, Spellmount, 2002

Butler, Rupert, *The Black Angels*, Arrow, 1989

Butler, Rupert, *Legions of Death*, Hamlyn, 1983

Forbes, Robert, *Pour L'Europe: The French Volunteers of the Waffen-SS*, self-published, 2000 (copy number 500)

Graber, G S, *History of the SS*, Diamond, 1994

Hastings, Max, *Das Reich: The March of the 2nd SS Panzer Division Through France 1944*, Pan, 1983

Jurado, Carlos Caballero, *Resistance Warfare 1940–45*, Osprey Men-at-Arms series, 1985

La Mazière, Christian de, *Ashes of Honor*, Tattoo, 1976

La Mazière, Christian de, *The Captive Dreamer*, Emperor Publishing e-book, 2004

Landwehr, Richard, *Charlemagne's Legionnaires: French Volunteers of the Waffen-SS*, Merriam Press e-book, 2003

Landwehr, Richard, 'The European Volunteer Movement of World War II', *Journal of Historical Review*, Vol. 2, No. 1, Spring 1981

Le Tissier, Tony, trans, *Berlin Dance of Death*, Spellmount 2005

Le Tissier, Tony, *With our backs to Berlin – The German Army in Retreat 1945*, Sutton, 2001

Mabire, Jean, *Mourir à Berlin*, Fayard, 1975

Mabire, Jean, *La Division Charlemagne*, Fayard, 1974

Quarrie, Bruce, *Hitler's Samurai,* Patrick Stephens, 1983
Reitlinger, Gerald, *The SS: Alibi of a Nation, 1939–1945,* Heinemann, 1956
Ripley, Tim, *Hitler's Praetorians: The History of the Waffen-SS 1925-1945,*
    Spellmount, 2004
Williamson, Gordon, *The Blood Soaked Soil,* Blitz Editions, 1997
Williamson, Gordon, *Loyalty is my Honor,* Brown, 1995
Williamson, Gordon, *The SS: Hitler's Instrument of Terror*, Spellmount, 2006

Index

Operation Barbarossa (invasion of
Soviet Union) 37, 51, 71, 134, 174
Operation Citadel (German Kursk
offensive 1943) 72
Operation Dynamo (Dunkirk
evacuation 1940) 30
Operation Market Garden (Allied
airborne Arnhem offensive 1944)
173
Operation Morocco (LVF anti-
partisan offensive 1944) 59
Operation Torch (Allied invasion of
North Africa 1943) 39
Operation Typhoon (German
offensive on Moscow 1941) 57
Operation Watch on the Rhine
(German Ardennes Offensive
1944-45) 132
Oradour-sur-Glane 13, 34, 60
Ordnungspolizei 47
Organization Todt 53, 129
Oschmann, General 59

panzerfäusts 13, 78-9, 110, 112-14,
142, 148-154
Panzer Meyer, Kurt 172
Papon, Maurice 163
Paris Commune 15
Parti Populaire Français (PPF) 17,
66, 77, 136
Parti Social Français (PSF) 16-7, 19,
66
Pavelic, Anté Dr (Croatias
Poglavnik) 50
Payras, Raymond 161
Pétain, Philippe Marshal 32-7, 59,
69
Peyron, Joseph 82
Photomaton 38
Pignard-Berthet, Paul 77, 117, 167
Phoney War 31

Poincaré, Raymond 18
Poland, invasion of 29
Popular Front Government (France)
16
Pomerania 76, 97-126, 129
Puaud, Edgar-Joseph-Alexandre
59, 85, 90, 102, 107, 110, 115, 118-
19
Puechlong, Jean-Louis 150
Puttkamer Strasse, battle of 150-51

Quisling, Vidkun 50

Radomysl, battle of 77-8
Rassemblement National Populaire
(RNP) 19, 67, 83
Raybaud, Emile 104, 111-12, 116,
167
Red Cross 24
Régiment de Marche (RM)
destruction of II/RM 119-21
formation of 116
Régiment de Reserve (RR)
destruction of 118-9
formation of 116
Reiche, Hans SS-Untersturmführer
79
Reichs Chancellery 11, 21, 139, 149-
151, 154, 156
Reichstag 11
Reichswehr 22, 25
Reynolds, Michael CB Major-
General retired 171
Ribbentrop, Joachim von 37
Rigeade, Yves 105, 120
Rosenberg, Alfred 48
Roque, de la Colonel 16
Röhm, Ernst 23-25
Rostaing, Pierre 27-8, 39, 62-3, 76,
81, 126, 137, 143-5, 155, 157, 166